Engineering Possibilities

Engineering Possibilities

Soft Skills for Young Engineers

Holly Blair

Engineering Possibilities by Holly Blair

ISBN-13: 978-1500982416

Charlie,

Thank you for interrupting my life.

Table of Contents

Preface

What's Possible?

Generally speaking, engineers are not known for their outstanding social skills. I can say this because I am an engineer. The thing is we weren't necessarily taught how to do that stuff— how to play the game. In university we stayed up late studying; we learned to apply complicated scientific principles and equations; we were overloaded with course work; we worked in groups with other like-minded engineering students; and in between all of that, most of us partied pretty hard. We made it through the program as a result of our persistence and hard work and earned ourselves an engineering degree. We were very proud of that degree and we set out to find a job in the real world.

Some of us found jobs right away; others went to graduate school to pursue our academic interests, or perhaps to extend our time as students and thus put off the day when we'd have to grow up and get a real job. At any rate, we eventually found our way into careers, in a variety of companies and in a variety of roles. We started working; weeks turned into months; months turned into years. At some point we realized that the skills that had made us successful in school were not the same as the skills that would make us

1

successful at work. Some of us stepped back, took a good look at ourselves, and said, "This is not the life I dreamed of. How did I get here?"

That's what happened to me, and not long after that moment of realization I found myself on an accelerated path of self-discovery. I didn't like what my life had come to, and I didn't know where it could possibly be headed. I knew I needed a change.

So I took action; and the more I learned, the more I realized how the things I was discovering could really benefit other young engineers who might be struggling to find their way.

Engineering school teaches you how to *think*. You might believe that engineering school teaches you how to do complicated math, complete detailed design projects, and calculate all the answers; but really, engineering school, no matter which college or university you attend, simply teaches you how to *think* – perhaps the most valuable skill taught in post-secondary institutions.

My best friend is Marilyn and she is 43 years older than me. She and her husband Bill became instant family friends when I was at the very impressionable age of 11. She worked for my dad as a Production Manager at a soup manufacturing plant, where he was her boss and the Plant Manager. Marilyn was very supportive and proud of me throughout my university years; however, she would always ask me when I was going to hurry up, get my piece of paper, and get out of there. I had a fantastic time in university and made lifelong friends, but school itself was not easy for me. I couldn't understand how she could possibly continue to relate my struggles and endless hard work to a simple piece of paper that was taking me a very long time to acquire. It wasn't until several years after I graduated with my hard-earned degree in chemical engineering that I finally realized what she meant by "my piece of paper."

Consider that your engineering degree is your ticket in—nothing more, nothing less. Any relevant work experience or being at the top of your graduating class is an asset, but definitely not a guarantee of success. There's a lot more to it than your hard technical skills, and this "stuff" is not taught in school. You have to learn it on your own, out in the real world, and for most people it's a true "trial by fire" exercise.

Being a particularly logical engineer, I tried to learn these "other" skills by reading a lot of books. I somehow believed that if I just read enough books, I'd find out all the answers and everything in my life would figure itself out. The truth was different: I had to discover the answers for myself through some pretty deep self-reflection. The books may have helped, but they didn't come close to providing the answers I was desperately searching for.

Then, after making significant progress in being authentic and true to myself, I discovered some astounding parallels between the things I was discovering and the underlying themes in some of my favorite children's books. It was a huge revelation. I used to know this stuff! I had somehow managed to forget it over the course of growing up, navigating my way through engineering school, and moving out on my own into the real world. It was humbling to realize that the six-year-old me used to *live* this stuff without hesitation or the need for comprehension! Smart girl...I guess at that age we're naturally self-expressed and connected with the real world.

I've gathered a collection of inspirational quotes, many from children's stories, and scattered them throughout this book, hoping that they resonate with you as much as they do with me. After all, you too were once curious and impressionable six-year-olds.

This book is written out of the possibility of compassion and connection, to help guide young engineers along their journey into the real world. It provides insight into the actions and behaviors you can choose, both at work and in your life, to bring about a sense of balance and ultimately a feeling of fulfillment and success. It's not necessarily a guide to getting to the top of the corporate ladder as fast as possible; rather, I hope that it inspires you to reflect on what's most important to you and discover the things that make you feel most alive, and that it encourages you to create a life you love.

There's a lot to this game called life. This book is a collection of the stories, quotes, tools and tricks that have helped me along my journey and that I want to share with you in hopes that they will make your own journey easier. Understand that there is no "end" to this journey; there is no 'destination.' It's about learning to enjoy the ride.

If you don't like something, change it.
If you can't change it, change your attitude.

– Maya Angelou[1]

Chapter 1

Discovering Your Passions

I've noticed that the most successful and happiest people seem to have something in common and that is that they are deeply passionate about something going on in their lives. They've identified their *purpose* in life and have structured their life around fulfilling that purpose. These individuals are lit up and excited when they're talking about what they're up to and they want to share it with everyone around them. You are passionate about something, you just have to first discover it and know that it may not be your career.

I've also noticed that the first step in discovering your passion is to *know yourself*, to really understand what it means to be authentic with yourself. There are a lot of significant and often unconscious expectations placed on young people today, and it can take some serious self-reflection to uncover our authentic selves. These external turned internal expectations arise from several areas: your parents, your upbringing, society, or even your peers. Once you are in touch with your authentic self, you get to make a choice on whether certain behaviors arise from external expectations placed on you or are really expressions of your true, authentic self. All of us have hard lessons to learn and things to sort out for ourselves. Some lessons are easier than others; it just depends on the situation, our past experiences, and how far we've ventured off the path. The exciting thing is that when you do figure things out and get back to being your real self, it feels as if *the whole world opens up to you*. So keep at it, the results are well worth the effort! Ultimately, being authentic is simply about being real.

> *"Real isn't how you are made," said the Skin Horse. "It's a thing that happens to you. When a child loves you for a long, long time, not just to play with, but REALLY loves you, then you become Real." "Does it hurt?" asked the Rabbit. "Sometimes," said the Skin Horse, for he was always truthful. "When you are Real, you don't mind being hurt." "Does it happen all at once, like being wound up," he asked, "or bit by bit?" "It doesn't happen all at once," said the Skin Horse. "You become. It takes a long time. That's why it doesn't happen often to people who break easily, or have sharp edges, or who have to be carefully kept. Generally, by the time you are Real, most of your hair has been loved off, and your eyes drop out and you get loose in the joints and very shabby. But these things don't matter at all, because once you are Real you can't be ugly, except to people who don't understand."*
>
> – Margery Williams, *The Velveteen Rabbit*[1]

Learning to be true to your authentic self, to be *who you really are*, is to let go of all the preconceived ideas and expectations you have unknowingly placed on yourself in the past and identify the ones that truly define you. It's letting go of all of your limiting beliefs and really allowing yourself to just be. Understand that your beliefs are shaped by your experiences, and therefore will change over time. They are dynamic, not static. It may not be easy, but discovering your authentic self makes everything you do in life much simpler. You'll know you've found it when you feel at ease, when all the craziness that we call our lives becomes calm and peaceful or zen.

Discovering your authentic self inevitably involves dealing with some tough stuff, all those thoughts and feelings you've previously been ignoring. You were ignoring them for a reason, so dig deep and discover what those reasons are. I guarantee you that the effort is worth the pain. I believe that recognizing your true authentic self, and then allowing yourself to just be yourself, is the last piece to becoming an adult. I'm totally confident that I'm not the only twenty-something who has wrestled with these ideas. Lift up the carpet of your life. What exactly have you been willing to sweep under there? Go deal with that stuff, because taking action is the only way to make a difference in those areas.

Along the path to discovering your authentic self, you may have the opportunity to participate in formal personality testing as an avenue for team building at work or in other settings. While these tests can provide valuable information regarding your understanding of how your actions and behaviors affect other people, you should be somewhat wary of the results. These tools have the potential to lead you into believing that you are what is written in the report. You might unconsciously find yourself living up to the identity created by the test results, perhaps out of a perceived need to fit into a particular role. Remember that these types of tools merely describe aspects of who you are; they don't *define* who you are. As you grow in your career and in your life, these descriptions also change over time because your work and your life experiences shape your behaviors and your beliefs. Use these personality profiles as helpful tools, not as definitions of who you are.

Next stop on the path: have you ever considered what *type* of engineer you are? Sure, there's chemical, mechanical, civil, electrical, and all the others, but what kind of engineer are you really? From my observations, there is a spectrum of skill sets that define the types of engineers. On one side, there are the strategic engineers, and on the other end of the spectrum, the more tactical engineers; in other words, big picture-oriented or task-oriented. Developing an understanding of where your strengths lie early in your career is an asset, as you will then be able to identify roles within your organization that best fit your abilities. Strategic engineers love to create a vision from their ideas and then develop a plan or strategy to make their vision a reality. They typically display strong leadership traits and are able to work well with others to achieve a common goal. Tactical engineers, on the other hand, really enjoy the more task-based approach. While I'm not saying they don't care about the bigger picture, they simply get more of their emotional satisfaction from completing the tasks that ultimately drive them to the end result. The tactical engineers are the detailed people, the ones that occasionally can't see the forest for all the trees, but who also roll up their sleeves and get things done.

Companies and technical organizations need both types of engineers to be successful; they need people with great vision and great strategic skills and they need people who then jump in and do the work. Too many strategists and nothing actually gets completed. Too many tactical experts, and while you may produce a lot of work, no one will have a grasp of the big picture. Both situations are a potential recipe for disaster. Another key point is that one type of engineer can't be successful without the other and they both need to be good at communicating and collaborating. Fortunately, most engineers aren't on the extreme ends and fall somewhere along the spectrum between big picture and detail oriented, but it's essential that you understand the difference and understand where your talents and abilities are best applied.

Try things out and learn which style you prefer; understand which type you identify closest with and build your career plan from there. This understanding of your talents and preferences will be an asset in your career and in your life. You will have the power to shape your career to fit your authentic self, which is much easier than trying to shape yourself to fit your career. The way I see it, there is no endpoint to get to in life; there are only choices to make along the way. Every door, every opportunity, is a choice. Pick one that interests you and give it a try. If things turn out well, great! If things aren't as awesome as you might like, don't worry; there is always another door to try. If you don't succeed on your first try, don't allow your fears to stop you from trying again. Keep going; embrace the journey.

Now take some time and think about what truly inspires you, or what has inspired you in the past. Have you ever seen something that made you want to get busy and do something about it? Something that really piqued your interest, made you smile, lit you up, or made you want to help? If yes, then you know how powerful that inspiration can be. So think about it, and look for those opportunities in life.

I've always been a curious person, wanting to understand exactly how things work. One of the most wondrous and extraordinary things I've ever witnessed was the day I watched the Atlantis space shuttle launch from Cape Canaveral, Florida. I'd watched lots of shuttle launches on TV, and when the opportunity arose to see one of the last NASA shuttle launches in person, I took it. I went to Florida for a few days with one of my close friends specifically to see the launch. We knew that several other launches had been rescheduled, and our trip could not accommodate any schedule changes. Knowing this, we had resolved that we would make multiple attempts to see a launch, as

11

this particular Atlantis flight was one of five last-ever shuttle launches and it was the final mission for Atlantis.

We set ourselves up to watch the launch along the causeway with several hundred other eager visitors, about six miles from the shuttle on the launch pad. We have one pair of binoculars, which are definitely required, as the launch pad is so far away. We learn that there is a dead zone for a couple of miles surrounding the shuttle, where people are not allowed to be due to hazardous exhaust gases from the rockets. I think to myself that this hazard is likely exaggerated, that there is probably a generous safety margin involved in the calculation of where we civilian spectators are ultimately located.

Finally, as it gets closer to launch time, I grow more and more worried that it will be cancelled. It's not until about 30 seconds before the launch that I realize this is actually going to happen and that I am here to see it! The countdown draws down to one; the liquid oxygen and booster rockets fire; the ground shakes (all 6 miles away and I suddenly have a massive appreciation for the safety zone distance); I can feel the power being exerted and it takes off. The shuttle leaves the Earth at a remarkable speed and heads into the sky, up into the darkness. I remember standing on the ground staring up into the clouds, just in awe of what I had witnessed—there were people inside that rocket and they had just left the planet!! Talk about a feat of engineering! I was inspired!

Once we got home, our friends told us that there had been only a 60 percent chance of launch that day.

There had been low-lying clouds earlier that morning and NASA had considered scrubbing the launch. Luckily, the weather had cleared up, and we got to see what was, for me, the most astoundingly awesome sight of my life!

What are you passionate about? What makes you feel alive and excited about life? There was a time that I really struggled with identifying my passions. I honestly thought that only *other* people got passionate about things and I just wasn't like that. Over time, I learned that I was actually not allowing myself to feel passionate because that would require me to be vulnerable, and obviously that was much too scary. Opening up, letting go and allowing myself to be vulnerable has been huge for me; the biggest thing that I've realized is how passionate I am about creating connections with other people, about sharing compassion and helping others succeed. This was a major revelation for me as I had been living my life rather aimlessly. No wonder I had been unhappy being so independent and stubborn!

Decide in your heart of hearts what really excites and challenges you, and start moving your life in that direction.

– Chris Hadfield, Canadian Astronaut[2]

Chapter 2

The Difference Makers: Soft Skills for Engineers

So what exactly are soft skills? I like to define them as the intangible, non-technical, touchy-feely-fuzzy stuff that can greatly contribute to a person's success in a way that goes beyond their purely technical capabilities. Soft skills can come very naturally to some engineers, while others, who may fit the stereotypical definition of an engineer more closely, struggle in this area. The good thing is that soft skills can be learned, developed and mastered over time and become strengths. You just have to be open to trying out new behaviors and discovering what works best for you.

What are the differences between hard skills and soft skills? Hard skills have measurement standards and their application generally results in an answer; one example is math. Soft skills are harder to quantify, and while they're difficult to measure, it can be very obvious when one person has certain soft skills and another person doesn't. Soft skills apply in all areas of your life, whereas hard skills tend to be more focused on a specific subject or area. There are fewer rules when learning and developing your soft skills. Unlike with hard technical skills, the development of soft skills doesn't have an endpoint. Rather, they are more like a talent or a continual journey of self-improvement.

Learning soft skills has no set curriculum or structure; as a young engineer you're typically left to figure things out on your own. On top of that, the skills you need to develop and master are unique to each individual. It's definitely a recipe for confusion. Some examples of soft skills competencies are listed in the following table under four overall headings:

Integrity	Leadership
• Accountability • Ownership • Authenticity • Personal Values • Work Ethic • Respect for Others • Commitment • Honesty • Reliability • Ethics • Morals	• Balance • Persistence • Communication • Listening • Vision • Teamwork • Being Inclusive • Negotiation • Setting Priorities • Decision-Making • Conflict Resolution
Power & Influence	**Continuous Improvement**
• Self Confidence • Creativity • Motivation • Perseverance • Assertiveness • Influence with, and without Authority • Critical Thinking • Time Management • Troubleshooting & Problem Solving	• Growth Mindset • Openness • Self-Discipline • Resilience • Optimism • Self-Awareness • Adaptability • Flexibility • Emotional Intelligence • Enthusiasm

Integrity

The definition of integrity is often associated with ethics and morals, with being right or wrong; but I'll argue that this is only a partial definition. To me, integrity is about keeping your word and doing what you know to be right without being righteous. Integrity also applies when something was not communicated directly to you, but only implied or simply expected. Integrity is about having the self-discipline to do what you know to be right when no one is watching.

Consider that integrity is something that you *are*, not something that you *have*. For that reason, a person can only *demonstrate* their integrity, not *speak* about their integrity. When someone is presented with or does something that is not in line with their personal integrity, they subconsciously know it; it's just a question of whether or not they realize that.

Leadership

Leadership is the ability to guide and direct a group of people towards a common goal. Great leaders provide the vision and pathway for groups of people to be successful. Leadership is about vision, teamwork, and effective communication. Making decisions, having vision, setting priorities, and having the ability to negotiate with others are important skills for leaders to have and to cultivate. Leadership is learning to understand other people's interests, skills and motivations, and then empowering them to live up to their potential and to discover and develop ideas of their own.

Power & Influence

Power and influence soft skills lie in your ability to take action and get things done—things that are in alignment with your goals and objectives. This includes the ability to delegate, motivate and influence *other people* to get things done. Engineers can sometimes fall victim to overanalyzing problems and fall into a state of 'analysis paralysis.' Your power and influence soft skills are the tools you use to break through being stuck and then take action.

I believe that everyone has the ability to create and be responsible for their own life; it's simply a matter of taking personal responsibility for the outcomes you desire and doing so in a powerful way. Being self-aware and understanding how much effort is "good enough" to achieve the desired outcome is a skill that can be learned over time and can be very powerful. Having the power within yourself to see what is possible in the face of obstacles requires a certain level of self-confidence and assertiveness. It's about understanding your own capabilities and the capabilities of the resources available, and then persevering to achieve results.

Continuous Improvement

While Integrity, Leadership, and Power & Influence form the basis of soft skills, Continuous Improvement soft skills are about having the inherent drive to learn, grow and develop your self. It's about being open to positive change, seeing what's possible, and staying resilient in the face of adversity. The spirit of continuous improvement is really the never-ending pursuit of excellence.

Before you can really dive into the deep end of the self-improvement swimming pool, you want to be prepared. Once you begin this journey, it really helps to be committed to becoming something greater. If your experience is anything like mine, you will quickly find yourself in deep self-reflection, questioning the ideas and beliefs that you previously understood to be utterly and completely true. Being authentically open to what you are about to recognize in yourself is imperative to generating the results that can arise from honestly questioning what you are up to in life. It's awkward and it's difficult, but I encourage you to embrace those emotions and work your way through to the other side, whatever that looks like. It's a scary process to consciously submit yourself to, and in my experience, it's absolutely worth the trouble.

Possibly the biggest thing that I've come to understand on my journey of self-discovery is that who I am to others is up to *me*, that how I present myself to the world is my own choice. I used to think that things just happened to me, and that I reacted to the situations in my life. I was *surviving* my life, not *living* my life. Coming to the realization that I am what I choose evolved into really understanding my authentic self, and it immeasurably increased my self-confidence. You may not even be aware of all the choices you make, but know that every conscious and unconscious choice you make in life actually defines who you are and how you live your life. Therefore you have the opportunity to create and design your own life. You get to be and do anything you want, so why not enjoy it? Consider for a moment that everything you've ever experienced has been a product of your own choices; and this goes for both the good and bad outcomes. Once you have that understanding, you have the power to choose the way you want to be and you're on your way to becoming an unstoppable force.

Another important concept that can provide clarity to your life is to understand the difference between making a *choice* and making a *decision*. Many people don't recognize the difference, but the difference has major implications for the way you approach your life.

To make a decision about something is to come to a solution or a conclusion, or to determine the best option, usually by exercising personal or professional judgment. Making a decision implies that one option is better or more attractive or more right than all the other possible options. Decisions bring with them implications of right or wrong, of good or bad; and decision-making is a very important skill for a young engineer to develop in the early stages of their career.

Making a choice, on the other hand, is the act of freely making a selection from different options or possibilities, after the consideration of any implications and consequences that your choice might carry. You are free and able to choose whatever you like, simply because you can. I've come to define the terms decision and choice as follows:

Decision: to solve or conclude; to determine or settle through consideration.

Choice: to select freely from a number of possible options, after consideration.

In the workplace, choices and decisions are made on a daily basis, often with important and high-value implications. When you find yourself in a situation where you are presented with multiple options, first understand whether you need to make a decision or a choice. If it's a decision, apply your best judgment. If you are being asked to make a choice, choose freely and be happy with the choice you make.

Another powerful piece of the concept of choice is that you have the ability to choose *everything* in your life. Good or bad, you can choose. The big difference here lies in your response to the situations that arise in your life. You'll naturally lean toward choices you like, but life doesn't always play along. There is great power to be found in choosing the less than ideal situations that life delivers. Bad bosses, troubled relationships, accidents or difficult assignments – when you accept them for what they are and consciously *choose* these things, you place yourself at the source of the issues. Then through taking action you allow yourself to move through the difficult situations more freely because, after all, it was your choice to experience those less than ideal things. The difference between making a decision or a choice represents a subtle shift in your mindset and offers you access to having peace of mind in your life.

Along the lines of making decisions or choices, having *acceptance* in your life is also very powerful. I would encourage you to give up on your inherent and unconscious need to create meaning of everything in your life and try out the ideas presented simply as the ideas that they are. When describing a situation in your life as "it is what it is," you're acknowledging the situation as it happened while being present to consequences and implications of the situation as they are right now. This little saying has a great amount of power to get you present to how well something is or isn't working. From that point of view, your attention is removed from what you perceive as being right or wrong with the situation, and spinning it around to see what good can be made of it going forward. It's truly accepting the situation as it is, being okay with that, and then being bold enough to move forward.

Applying these ideas of choices, decisions and acceptance in your life can result in a positive shift in your mindset. Life can be something that happens to you, or you can choose to be responsible for yourself and create your own life just the way you want it to be.

You've always had the power, my dear.
You've had it all along.

– Glinda, the Good Witch, *The Wizard of Oz*[1]

Chapter 3

What Do You Want To Be When You Grow Up?

Soft Skills Focus: Authenticity, Vision, Setting Goals and Creativity

Throughout my childhood, there were a total of three things I wanted to be when I grew up. They changed every few years, and in the end I chose engineering. My first idea was actually a secret desire, as no one in my family remembers me telling them this. At a young age I apparently knew that some career choices required a longer and more difficult path than others and so I discounted my secret desire before it could begin, to the point that I never even told anyone about it. The first thing I remember that I wanted to be when I grew up was an astronaut. I expect this idea had to do with something I saw on TV and was well aligned with my inherent curiosity and sense of adventure. At any rate, even if I had told anyone about my dream job, my hopes would have been cut short pretty quickly: when I was six years old, my parents discovered I was color blind.

Later, around age ten or eleven, I wanted to be a writer. I enjoyed being creative and developing characters and telling stories. I really enjoyed reading as a child (and also as an adult) and thought it would be cool to write stories for other people to read. I'm not sure when or why I dropped this notion, but even before entering high school, I made up my mind that I was going to become an engineer. My dad was an engineer, I was good at math and science, and I was endlessly curious.

As it turned out, engineering was a good fit for me. I really enjoy being an engineer, especially when it comes to the practical aspects of the job. The majority of my career to date has been spent working in chemical plants, closely involved in daily plant operations.

Think about the things you wanted to be one day. Is there anything hidden within those memories that still inspires you today? I'm not saying that you weren't supposed to be an engineer, just that there could be more hiding there than you give yourself credit for. As we grow up, we unconsciously develop limiting beliefs based on our experiences and the various expectations placed upon us by others. Trying to separate what you really want from what you or others think you should want or should be can be a tricky exercise, as those beliefs are often deeply ingrained and almost invisible. Look closely; maybe there's something from when you were small that you have forgotten about and that would make you feel alive if you were able to do it today. Maybe it's worth pursuing as a hobby or interest, or maybe you should take some classes at a local college or volunteer in that area. What makes your heart sing?

Now think about why you first wanted to become an engineer. Was there a particular time or event in your life that first piqued your interest? Was there ever a time that you were inspired by someone you met or maybe someone you read about? Engineering is a difficult program, so first think about why you chose it, and then why you stuck with it. Get present to those ideas and reasons, and then set out about creating yourself a career you love with your newfound understanding of yourself. An engineering degree is your ticket into the work place, and from there, it's up to you to decide what type of work to do. The cool thing about an engineering degree is how versatile it is and the multitude of opportunities it can offer you. If you're not sure what to do straight out of school, know that most large organizations offer early career rotation programs. These programs offer you the opportunity to try out a variety of roles in different departments and locations within a period of a few years. Consider taking advantage of such a program and try out different jobs. Your choice of career just might surprise you when you're finished the rotation program.

Successful people are intentional in their behaviors and actions. They know what they are up to; they are playing the game of life and they're actively engaged in it. Consider that if you don't know where you want to go, how will you ever know that you're headed in the right direction?

> *Would you tell me, please, which way I ought to go from here?" "That depends a good deal on where you want to get to," said the Cat. "I don't much care where..." said Alice. "Then it doesn't matter which way you go," said the Cat. "...so long as I get somewhere," Alice added as an explanation. "Oh, you're sure to do that," said the Cat, "if only you walk long enough.*

– Lewis Carroll, *Alice's Adventures in Wonderland*[1]

Being intentional in your behaviors and actions starts with creating a possibility of where you want to get to and what you want to become in your life. When you begin with the end in mind, it creates a sense of purpose and direction in your life that drives you to achieve success. Be careful to avoid becoming complacent in this journey. Take time periodically to reset and evaluate your progress toward your goals and reflect on the goals themselves. It's okay to change and adjust your direction as you go along; the important thing is to maintain forward momentum.

One way of driving forward momentum in your life is to consistently challenge yourself. That is, be brave and do the things that scare you. Recognize your fear of being wrong, of looking dumb, of not being good enough – whatever it is that's stopping you – and take action in spite of those fears. Everyone has fears like and everyone gets stopped in their life from time to time. Consider that the things you desire the most are on the other side of your fears.

If you get stuck in life or feel like you've fallen into a rut, there are ways to quickly bring yourself back on track. First, acknowledge being stuck and look to understand the impact that your being stuck is having on your life. What is missing from your life as a result of being stuck? Identify the aspects of the impact on your life that you are not okay with. Once you can see the impact and the consequences of being stuck, you create a driving force for positive change. Then, the only thing that can make a difference in those areas of your life is for you to take action, however small, towards your greater goal. Force yourself to do the things that scare you in life; it's how you get the results you really want.

To help you focus your direction in your self-development journey, the concept of SMART goals can be applied. SMART goals are Specific, Measureable, Achievable, Relevant and Time Bound[2].

Specific – What exactly do you want to achieve? Use very specific language to describe the outcome or result you desire.

Measurable – How will you gauge success if you can't measure the improvement? Consider how you will demonstrate achievement of the goal. Make up your own measurement system if necessary.

Achievable – What's possible in the area you're looking to improve? Consider goals that support movement in the right direction, and always strive for competency over perfection. I would encourage you to be unreasonable with the term "achievable." Set out from the beginning to do the things that you're not immediately sure you can do.

Relevant – How are your goals aligned to your role at work or to your life? Which strategic objectives are they in direct support of? Be very clear on the relevancy of your goals; this is vitally important.

Time Bound – Define when you will complete your goal. The timely achievement of your goals is important to your success. Declare the month, day or year of the completion date of your goal.

In your work, set goals for yourself frequently, even if that occurs outside of your company's performance management program. Having personal goals for your life outside of work is also an important exercise, as it will help you to achieve that feeling of balance when you know you're moving towards something great. Remember that you alone are in charge of yourself, so understand that the responsibility for goal setting and performance management sits squarely with you. Start small – goals don't have to be big and daunting. They can be simple things, like improving your presentation skills or leading a small group of people in a troubleshooting exercise. Success, after all, is doing a common thing uncommonly well.

Look for opportunities within your realm of influence to practice your skills. Volunteer to give presentations in support of a new initiative your group is rolling out to the department; ask your supervisor if you can take the lead on a small project related to your role; or volunteer to help out with a company fundraiser or celebration. There are lots of opportunities available to you if you pay attention.

Chapter 4

Learn to Manage Yourself First

Soft Skills Focus: Self-Awareness, Emotional Intelligence, Resilience and Self-Confidence

The ability to effectively manage yourself includes motivating yourself, taking initiative, and proactively solving your own problems. It's about emotional intelligence – the ability to be aware of your own emotions and use them effectively.

Learning to manage yourself first is all about developing your sense of self-awareness. Whether you realize it or not, you alone are in control of *you*, and of how you relate to other people and situations in your life. This goes back to the idea that everything you do in life is a choice you make, but now we're going deeper and saying that who you are and who you want to be is your choice as well. A lot of things can happen in life, and how you perceive those things is completely up to you. Life can happen *to* you or life can happen *for* you.

Self-awareness is the understanding of how your behaviors and actions affect other people. It's an observation tool that allows you to see the impact of your interactions with other people and then you can make changes. Consider that everyone has blind spots regarding how they interact with other people, things they aren't able to see for themselves, things that could be in support of or be detrimental to their success in life. What you don't know you don't know can limit you, or even hurt you. The usual way to find out what your blind spots are is to ask other people. While your own blind spots are impossible for you to see, they can be incredibly obvious to other people, particularly those closest to you in life. The secret is to be brave, ask others for feedback on your performance, and (this is the key part), be open to actually listening to what they have to say about you. Remember that their feedback is only their perception of you, not necessarily the way that you really are or how you might have intended to come across. Take what others tell you about yourself and try to apply their feedback in a positive way.

I've always been an independent person. From a very young age I've wanted to do things myself. My mom says I was a particularly driven toddler, often getting frustrated when I needed help with something. Being independent can be a positive trait depending on how you apply it in your life. One of my blind spots that I realized along the way due to feedback from others was that my strong sense of independence had actually become somewhat detrimental to my success.

I had developed a belief that it was absolutely better to do things myself, discounting the need to properly communicate with others, to a point that it occurred to other people that I was acting as if it was me against the world. In short, I was becoming difficult to work with. Once I really saw the impact of my behavior, I was able to make different choices and take different actions. I became more understanding of others and much more open to collaboration.

In my experience, when you go out of your way to ask for feedback from people, they are more than willing to give you constructive criticism because they can see your commitment to learn and grow. In return, they may ask you to provide feedback for them. Be careful of providing unsolicited criticism to others, as they may not be as open to self-improvement as you are. You'll be surprised how far these real conversations will take your working relationship with that person. Basically, to grow and develop yourself, you have to learn how to be comfortable being uncomfortable. Lean into the uncertainty and see what happens. Nothing great ever came from staying in your comfort zone.

Once we accept our limits, we go beyond them.

– Albert Einstein[1]

Another major aspect of being self-aware is developing an understanding and appreciation of your limiting beliefs. Limiting beliefs are things you have learned to believe that prevent you from seeing what could be possible. You develop them unconsciously through your life experiences, what you think about yourself, and what other people tell you about yourself. The scariest part is that you almost always can't see these limiting beliefs yourself, yet you are allowing them to run your life. If you're as delusional as I was, you might even think you don't have any limiting beliefs; that you already know yourself too well to have any. Save yourself the breakdown and consider that you might have at least one or two.

Another way to describe limiting beliefs is that they are like filters through which you view the world. They're constructed and developed from your thoughts and perceptions of the world around you. Consider that your limiting beliefs could unconsciously be causing you to live at a level below your true potential.

Two ways of identifying and recognizing your limiting beliefs include examining patterns and looking at what you are expecting from different situations in your life. You'll probably notice that you have certain behaviors and actions that are actually causing you to repeat the past over and over again in different forms. There are likely examples of when you searched out supporting ideas and examples to justify your beliefs, or you might regularly seek out the meaning of situations and events that relate to and are aligned with your beliefs. You likely have a habit of judging and evaluating everything you experience as it fits into what you already know and believe. Check yourself on this habit; it might not be serving you.

Everyone has these types of limiting beliefs. They arise from our past and from lessons we've learned in life. They're designed to protect us and we think they're in place to help us. I would encourage you to take a look at your beliefs and ask yourself how they are serving you. You might find that some of the things you routinely think have you stuck thinking you can't do something for some reason, that there are certain things that are impossible for you to achieve. Some examples of common limiting beliefs are:

It didn't work last time, so why bother to try.

I can't be active because I'm not an athlete.

I'm not good enough to have that in my life.

I don't know what I'm doing so I'm not going to try.

I don't want to get hurt so I'll just play it safe.

Notice that your limiting beliefs follow a pattern: I can't, don't or shouldn't do X, because of Y. We can rationalize and justify what we think and we know that for us, these can be absolute truths. We have proven to ourselves exactly how they are true for us and develop strategies to work around them. Consider that you might even be resigned to the idea that they could ever possibly change.

One of my earliest limiting beliefs became deeply engrained when I was six years old. It was track and field day at school and all the kids in my class were running the 100-meter dash on the track behind the school. I remember being in last place by a really long way but I was having fun running around and I really didn't care that I was so far behind the other kids. The gym teacher came over to me and said, "It's okay, Holly, you don't have to do this. You can go over there and sit on the hill and wait for the other kids to finish." I stop running and for the first time I realize there is something wrong with what I am doing, and worse yet – there is something wrong with me. I go over to the hill and sit down by myself. I probably cried but what I really remember is being confused. My little six-year-old brain is spinning, trying to figure out what I had been doing wrong. In that moment I conclude that I am not good at running and not good at gym class. I desperately want to be good at something and since this is apparently not it, I feel I have to choose something different to be very good at in order to hide my weakness. I choose math. What's more, I not only want to be good at math; I want to be the best. I set out right then at six years old, all upset sitting alone on a hill in my gym clothes that I am going to become the smartest kid in school.

I held onto this ideal and placed high expectations on myself to be perfect for the rest of my academic career. This identity creating belief has served me very well and garnered great success for me in my life. However these ideas have also limited me in what I believed possible for myself in terms of my health and wellness later as an adult. It's only been recently that I've seen the ridiculousness of my six-year-old self's decision and made new commitments in my life around being more athletic and healthier, and to be okay without the need for perfection.

If you recognize some of your beliefs as being limiting beliefs, particularly around what is and isn't possible for yourself in life, ask yourself to carefully examine the facts. Are you perhaps manufacturing additional stories and meanings and adding those to the facts? How are these actions helping you? How are these actions hurting you? Which parts of your story about what happened are actually true?

Another thing to be conscious of is your self-talk. I'm referring to the little voice in your head that decides what is and isn't possible for you. Be mindful of how you are speaking to yourself. Your self-talk has the power to stop you in your tracks or to cause you to believe that anything is possible.

Negative self-talk is something I became exceptionally good at. I had an underlying and hidden limiting belief that I wasn't good enough for the things I wanted the most in my life. When things did work out the way I hoped, I thought I had just gotten lucky, that things were good in that situation but that it was absolutely a one-time occurrence. I had a belief that life was hard and that I needed to struggle to get by. But I wouldn't let people see that struggle and I kept it very private. I very rarely asked anyone for help.

Pay attention to the choice of words that you're making in your communication with yourself. Are there a lot of definitive words like never, always, and can't, or are you having a more open and understanding conversation? Do you continually think you're not good enough? How nice are you being to you? One way I've found to quickly stop this negative pattern is to find a picture of yourself when you were a child and put it in your phone. When you find yourself engaged in negative self-talk, look at the picture and ask yourself if you would say those same things to that little child. Chances are you wouldn't. I find that this is an incredibly effective way to quickly shift my energy to the positive.

If you find yourself engaged in the negative self-talk conversation of "I can't do something," stop and ask yourself, "Why not?" If you were to acknowledge your feelings of inadequacy and then do the thing you think you can't do anyway, what's really the worst that could happen? Try being brave and pushing yourself to do the impossible, and just see what happens.

I used to have a nasty habit of making myself very busy in an effort to distract myself from the fact that I was not taking action in my life to achieve the things I really wanted, and that I was actually afraid to try. I didn't want to acknowledge that to myself so I found ways to keep busy to avoid dwelling on those fears. I took up all sorts of activities, some of which I did enjoy, but I was doing them for all the wrong reasons. They were all things that gave me pleasure, the fleeting form of happiness.

I would entertain my love of skiing by going to the mountains as much as possible. Skiing was an activity that forced me to be present and in the moment; it made the little voice in my head stop over-analyzing everything in my life. It was quiet in the mountains and I needed to have that in my life.

I became a serial work-alcoholic, tying my identity to my job. I consciously hid from the areas of my life that weren't working very well; at work, I felt I could control things and create success for myself. I was good at my job but it wasn't making me as happy as I had expected it to.

Outside of work I would do things that were actually detrimental to my success in life, my life balance and my well-being. This included being somewhat reckless with my money, continuing to participate in activities even though I was injured, drinking more than I should, going along with things just because my friends were doing them and I didn't want to miss out. Finally, I realized that the person I was hurting the most with these behaviors was me.

I got some help and then I got some coaching on how to recognize the error in some of my more self-deprecating behaviors and how to change the way I was talking with myself so as to cultivate a more positive mindset. Over time I learned that I could choose to make myself happy or I could choose to make myself sad. My life started to turn around.

We either make ourselves miserable or we make ourselves strong. The amount of effort is the same.

– Carlos Castenada[2]

There is a common trap that many engineers fall into – perfectionism. This was something I was absolutely guilty of. Perfectionism is the need to handle all possible situations with ease, complete all assignments, meet all deadlines, know the answer to every question, in order to live a happy and fulfilling life – the need to have it all. You actually can have it all, but as I've come to learn, you don't get there by being perfect. Perfectionism is like a trap that lets you get just close enough to see your end goal, but never quite close enough to achieve it. The harsh reality is that striving for perfectionism will hurt you more than it will help you. Create some boundaries for yourself and learn to understand what "good enough" looks like for you. A little hint: your "good enough" effort is equal to the best effort you are capable of; it's just about doing your best. A healthier strategy is to pursue *excellence*, not perfection.

Even the most self-aware individuals can't see everything they need to see about themselves, so ask people around you for feedback as often as you can. I've learned that who you see yourself to be and who others see what you are, is rarely the same person. You've probably heard this before, but it really is all about perception. Who you are to others only exists in their listening of you. Other people observe your ideas, actions and behaviors over time and naturally expect more of the same from you. When you change your ideas, actions or behaviors, others can often perceive you as doing something out of character.

Your new ideas might be more aligned to your authentic self, but it will come as a surprise to those around you. Take the time to have conversations with people in your life and have them express their perception of you. If you're truly open to hearing and appreciating their feedback, this can be an enlightening experience and you can learn some very interesting things about how others perceive you. From there, be authentic; share who you are as a possibility and watch as those people now see you and listen to you in a different light. Everyone has blind spots regarding how they are being or acting with other people. Regularly requesting feedback sheds light on those blind spots and has the potential to propel you forward in terms of your performance. Who knows, you might just realize that you've been acting insane.

Insanity: doing the same thing over and over again and expecting different results.

– Albert Einstein[3]

A common and destructive behavior displayed by some young engineers is an air of superiority, an enlarged ego regarding their abilities and worthiness in their chosen profession as an engineer. Granted, society says that to become an engineer is a noble choice, but that choice doesn't make your career choice any better than anyone else's. If you've fallen into this trap, consider the pattern of thoughts that led you to that conclusion, decide how important that view is to you, and think about adopting a different outlook. Your self-centered attitude isn't attractive to other people and it will hold you back in your career until you change your mindset. Learn to appreciate the opinions and experience of others, and be a team player. You have a degree in engineering; you do not know everything there possibly is to know.

Another behavior that will set you apart from others is the practice of minimizing and eliminating the wasteful activities of criticizing, condemning and complaining about people or issues in your life. Although easy to slip into, these three ordinary and negative behaviors hamper your effectiveness and ultimately your success. While you're busy criticizing, condemning or complaining about a situation, you're actually giving up your power to change and influence that situation for the better. Consider what could be possible if you dropped the consistent complaints and took action to improve those situations instead. You won't always agree with everything that is presented to you in life, but you can learn something from everything that is presented to you.

Any fool can criticize, condemn and complain, but it takes character and self control to be understanding and forgiving.

– Dale Carnegie, *How to Win Friends and Influence People*[4]

Personal and professional development should be thought of as a journey, not a destination. Developing your mastery of soft skills involves having the drive to continually improve and to periodically evaluate your progress. When you are working to develop your competence in a certain area, there are four stages of learning that everyone goes through on their way to mastery of that skill:

1. Unconscious Incompetence
2. Conscious Incompetence
3. Conscious Competence
4. Unconscious Competence

To demonstrate these four stages of learning a new skill or behavior, think back to when you were a kid learning to tie your shoelaces. At first you didn't know how to tie your shoes and you were probably okay with that. You didn't know you didn't know and you were already a pro at those Velcro straps anyway. Then, your parents made an effort to teach you and you entered the phase of conscious incompetence; you had an idea of how to tie your shoes but often did not succeed on your own and required help. Then one day you figured it out; those bunny ears became a bow and you were incredibly proud of yourself. You told everyone you could about your accomplishment. *Conscious competence.* Now, think about when you tied your shoelaces earlier today, chances are that mundane task didn't even faze you; it's become something for which you have *unconscious competence.* This same logic applies to larger, more complex real-world skills than looping the bunny ears around each other.

To end the discussion of self-awareness and learning to manage yourself, I'll share the most powerful quote that I was introduced to during the course of my own journey. It has to do with first realizing, and then appreciating, that where you are in life, wherever that is or however that looks, it is okay.

If you could really accept that you weren't okay,
You could stop proving that you were okay.
If you could stop proving that you were okay,
You could get it that it is okay to not be okay.
If you could get it that it was okay to not be okay,
You could get it that you were okay the way you are.
You are okay, get it?

– Werner Erhard[5]

Chapter 5

Understand Your Generational Identity

Soft Skills Focus: Growth Mindset, Work Ethic and Self-Awareness

If you're a young engineer today, then you're also a member of Generation Y, which is the generation defined as those individuals born in the 1980's and 1990's. While every person is completely unique with their own strengths and weaknesses, having an understanding of the generation you belong to can help you to develop an appreciation of the beliefs, strengths and weaknesses that were instilled into you as you grew up. It's also beneficial to appreciate the styles and skills of other generations of people that you work with.

Some positive characteristics and traits commonly associated with Generation Y, also known as the Millennial Generation, are that we're ambitious, well connected and open minded to more controversial ideas than our preceding generations. Collectively, we tend to thrive in collaborative environments where we get to actively contribute to solutions. We want to be involved with meaningful work early on in our careers and sometimes our high expectations for ourselves aren't readily met when we first enter the working world.

Our generation is highly educated and confident. We are generally willing to challenge authority to achieve something that we perceive as a greater good. We seek out regular feedback and often look for affirmation from others that we're doing a good job. Our communication style often defaults to the more disconnected emails and text messages rather than verbal and in-person conversations. Our presence within social networks keeps us well connected but can also lead to our participation in a dangerous game of constantly comparing ourselves and our level of success to that of our friends and peers.

We appreciate work life balance in a different way than older generations, placing more emphasis on our personal lives. While we are willing to work hard for things we believe in, we want to do it in our own way. Often, that means blurring the lines between our work and personal lives. Being overly connected means we have the ability to answer emails on our cell phones in the evenings, and we appreciate flexible work schedules to accommodate our many interests and ambitions outside of work. We're achievement oriented and we want to figure out the easiest way to have it all.

I've also heard our generation described as lazy, easily distracted young people obsessed with technology. These comments encompass a variety of stereotypes including that we don't appreciate the value of hard work, that we have unrealistically high expectations, expect instant gratification, and have low levels of commitment. I'll argue that the people who've made such comments haven't taken the time to get to know us. But by the same token, have we actually taken the time to get to know them?

There is a generational gap that exists in workplaces today, which is likely magnified by technology in the workplace and our immediate familiarity with it in comparison to older generations. When working with others in our jobs, it's important to be conscious of this generation gap. Our level of awareness of those differences dictates how we interact with others. This can be a strength we're recognized for, or if we don't acknowledge it, it could hinder our success.

Once, while working on a major project, I was routinely collaborating with a senior engineer who was working on a similar project at another plant. He and I had developed a presentation for upper management and we wanted to run it by the plant manager of the facility I was working at. I organized a meeting on short notice and brought my laptop with the presentation along to the meeting. As we're beginning the discussion with the plant manager, I realize that my computer won't turn on – technology is failing me. This unexpected breakdown throws me off and I stumble over my words. I *need* the file on the computer for our discussion. Out of nowhere, the senior engineer produces a paper copy of our presentation. He had printed it out, as it was his preference to use paper over technology. It had never occurred to me to print the file, yet it was second nature to him. Without him, our meeting would have come to a halt until I had the technology issues sorted out. Out of that experience, I learned to limit my reliance on technology in important conversations and that sometimes simpler is better; to genuinely appreciate the contributions of older generations in the work force.

Engineering, in particular, is a field where there is a significant amount of on-the-job learning. There's a reason you don't come out of school as a qualified engineer and why you're called an Engineer-in-Training. University only teaches you so much and is primarily focused on the theoretical aspects of the profession. You then have several years of on-the-job training to learn the more practical and more specific technical aspects of engineering. You gain competence in your engineering skills and also develop your engineering judgment by working closely with older and more experienced engineers and mentors. So be confident in yourself, be respectful of others, and always stay humble.

The only source of knowledge is experience.

– Albert Einstein[1]

Chapter 6

Operate With Integrity

Soft Skills Focus: Accountability, Honesty, Personal Values, Respect for Others, Ethics and Morals

I've noticed that having a fear of commitment is a very common limitation of young people. Commitment can be misunderstood as implying that there is a specific plan to follow, and that everything is decided according to that plan, and all you have to do is live it out. In a way, despite the intention of the word 'commitment,' it can feel very final, very relegated. So some people tend to shy away from it, to live their lives through minimizing their commitments in many different ways: choosing month-to-month rental agreements, avoiding cell phone contracts, refusing to think in the long term, jumping from job to job. It's like living your life in "wait and see" mode. Sometimes choosing this way of being can be exciting and exhilarating, and other times it feels directionless and perhaps even hopeless.

Consider that if you are experiencing a fear of commitment, it might actually be your integrity that is lacking. If you're enjoying your minimal commitment lifestyle, then all the power to you; you're living the way you want to be and that's fantastic. However, if the feeling stems from a true fear of commitment, consider the idea of committing to an idea or a possibility, rather than a specific plan to get back on track. Create the possibility of having a committed relationship in your life, or committing to a job working for an awesome company, or committing to going to the gym regularly, whatever it is you really want to do, even if it's vague at this point. If it begins as a possibility, it means it's not concrete yet; you can just let that possibility exist and unfold in one way or another. Create possibility even when what you're up to seems completely impossible.

It's kind of fun to do the impossible.

– Walt Disney[1]

When someone at work asks you a question, remember that "I don't know" is a perfectly good answer. No one ever expects you to know everything or have all the answers at any given time. They do, however, expect you to be open and honest. Don't compromise your integrity by saying something that is not, or may not be, true. It's much better to say you don't know and then go find out, rather than pretending you know and making something up to look like you are on top of everything. Be willing to be wrong, even if it means you won't look good to other people. If you're unclear about something, ask a question. Remember that the only dumb questions are the ones that you don't ask; it's always better to ask than to assume. Maintaining your integrity is how you keep things clean, how you develop and maintain trust and loyalty in your relationships with other people.

Along the same line, it's important to go about the business of building yourself a reputation for credibility. You can achieve a credible reputation by consistently delivering on your commitments and holding others accountable. Highly effective people understand the power of collaboration, and that the collective ideas of a team or a community can be a very powerful force. If someone shares a really good idea with you and you elevate it to a higher level, always return the credit for that idea to the person it originated from. Don't steal ideas from people. Instead, be a platform for people to share their thoughts and ideas with you. In doing this, you'll find that people are naturally much more willing to share important things with you. This skill of being approachable and trustworthy can be particularly valuable in difficult troubleshooting situations and will absolutely be recognized by the people around you.

Everyone makes mistakes, especially little ones. Even if it seems inconsequential, if you've told someone something that you later find out to be incorrect or untrue, go back and clean that up with them. Explain that you have found out more about the problem or issue at hand, and that the information you shared with them earlier is not correct. You will restore your integrity with that person and earn their trust by demonstrating your integrity and accountability.

For every action there is an equal and opposite reaction.

– Sir Isaac Newton, *Newton's Third Law*[2]

A major part of integrity is keeping your word with other people. When you really think about it, your word is all you have. We're all human and no one can keep their word in every area of their life all the time. Life happens, circumstances change, and promises sometimes get broken. When that happens, it's important to realize what happened and the impact that not keeping your word had on both yourself and the other people involved. Have a conversation with the people impacted by your actions; discuss the impact of not keeping your word and explain how you will prevent such an instance from happening in the future. Perhaps there is a system or process you can put in place that will hold you accountable in the future. In my experience, the process you could create could be as simple as setting a reminder alarm on your cell phone.

The proactive approach to a mistake is to acknowledge it instantly, correct and learn from it.

– Stephen Covey[3]

Life is messy and your integrity helps keep it clean. Imagine that your life is a game of dodge ball. To live a life with true integrity, you have to be willing to get hit by the ball. Be brave enough to give up the need to duck, dive and dodge the wrenches of life; to stand up and catch them instead. That's life by design.

Chapter 7

Communicate!

Soft Skills Focus: Communication, Negotiation and Being Inclusive

Communication can be challenging for engineers (and really for all people), and it can be particularly uncomfortable for those who tend to be more introverted personalities. Of all the soft skills, being able to communicate your ideas effectively is possibly the most important skill to master. You can be the smartest person in a group of people, but if you can't effectively share your ideas and collaborate with others, you won't get very far in your career or in your life.

Effective communication encompasses three main types of communication: verbal, non-verbal and written. Verbal communication includes speaking and, more importantly, listening. Non-verbal communication, arguably the most powerful type, includes body language, facial expressions and tone of voice. Formal and informal written communications make up the third type of communication. Each form of communication is unique, with different subsets of soft skills.

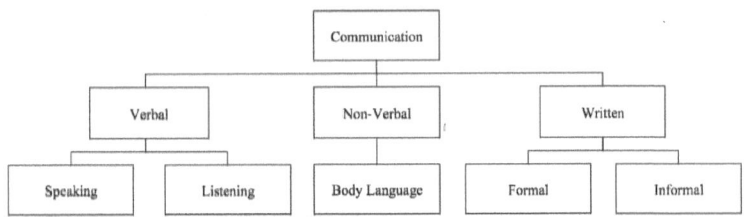

I believe that the foundation of effective communication is self-confidence. When your self-confidence is lacking, everyone can tell. You get nervous, your voice wavers, and you might tend to look down at the ground instead of at your audience. Luckily, self-confidence is something you can develop and increase with the application of a few simple tricks.

It's easier to be confident in your communication when you truly understand the material you're presenting, so first make sure you know what you're talking about. Don't speak out of turn or for other people. Maintain eye contact with the people in your audience when you are talking with them. Resist the urge to look down at your shoes—trust me, they're still there. Practice a good handshake; it should be firm and strong, not weak or floppy. Believe in yourself and your ideas—confidence is a state of mind.

When you want to share your ideas with other people and influence them, make a conscious effort to communicate with them in the way they would prefer.

The Golden Rule (do unto others as you would have them do unto you) does not apply here. It's all about the other person and the Platinum Rule applies instead: do unto others, as they would do unto themselves. This is of particular importance when directing your communication upwards in an organization. Take the time to study the person you're going to talk to and try to figure out their individual style of preferred communication. Do they like to study written material with lots of detail, do they get the most from formal presentations, or are they keen to engage in informal hallway discussions? Each person's communication style is different, and when you align your message to his or her preferred way of communicating, your ideas will be delivered most effectively. When considering how I would deliver a message to people working at levels above me, I used to put myself in the other person's place and consider what I would want to see from me if I was in their position. This approach proved only marginally successful, and it wasn't until I eventually realized that I wasn't actually communicating to myself that I saw my own mistake. At the time, this concept was revolutionary to me.

If you have a great idea, share it with everyone you can. Remember that no one can read your mind. Be inclusive, communicate and express your idea in all directions: up, down, sideways and across. Your idea will grow and develop every time you share it with other people, and soon you won't even recognize it— it will be that great. Even greater is to let your own idea go and allow it to be developed by other people as their own idea.

I once worked on a team with a great internal dynamic, in a role where I worked very closely with experienced operators to solve problems pertaining to daily plant operations. The issues we dealt with were immediate, high profile and seemed to never end. Over time, we learned to work together well, which made the role a lot of fun for me. With the more technical problems, there would be times when I'd jump ahead and assume the operations guys knew what I meant, forgetting that the guys I was working with hadn't gone to engineering school. While they knew the practical side of the plant operations much better than I did, I would sometimes leave them behind on the more technical issues. They'd stop me and say "Holly, you're talking Engineer to me again." It was the best thing I could have learned from them in that role: how to explain complicated technical issues in a way that anyone could understand—Operator Speak, as we came to call it. Being connected and relatable is one of the best strengths a young engineer can have, and if it doesn't come naturally to you, make an effort to focus on it and develop it. It will be well worth the effort.

If you can't explain it simply, you don't understand it well enough.

– Albert Einstein[1]

Written communication is another important skill for young engineers to master. Most written communication today is in the form of memos, technical reports and emails. It is important to limit your written communication to coherent, concise reports that provide sufficient detail, such that your reader can easily understand your work and then make an informed decision. If you write an email to someone and they have to use the scroll bar to read it, it's too long.

When you've been asked to provide a written report on a certain topic, before you start writing, presence yourself to the purpose of the communication you've been asked to provide. Consider the audience who will be reading your report and think about what they want to see from your analysis. Which specific findings are they most interested in? What exact information do they require from you to make their business decision? When in doubt, a simple clarification question is a good idea. Put your most important findings in an executive summary at the beginning of your document and reference the less relevant details in appendices. Some people want to see that you've covered the details, but most really only concern themselves with the final answer and just want to see that you've covered the bases.

In your written communication, you will probably be tempted to tell people the answers that you've figured out for them. A common pitfall for a young engineer is being attached to the outcome of their exact solution being implemented. It is very difficult to detach yourself sometimes, but try to simply *recommend* solutions to the people above you, rather than tell them what to do.

Some things, however, are worth being attached to. Personal safety, for example, is a core value of successful organizations, and that should not be compromised. However, if you're simply dealing with economic or other strategic decisions, try your best to not become attached to a particular outcome from your analysis. Instead, commit yourself to providing the reader the best information you can, so they can make an informed decision. This is a careful balance for young engineers, as making these decisions based on your data analysis helps to grow and develop your professional judgment. When they can, good leaders will engage you as a young engineer in their decision-making processes as an opportunity to learn, but this won't always be the case. If you're left out of their considerations, don't make that mean anything; next time ask if they might consider including you in their thinking process so you can develop your own critical thinking skills.

Finally, don't underestimate the significance of using proper spelling and grammar in your written communications. Both spelling and grammar are marks of professionalism and the unspoken impact of using either one incorrectly might surprise you. A lot of people hold spelling and grammar in high regard. If spelling isn't your forte, just be smart about it – use the spelling and grammar check functions, proofread your emails before hitting 'send,' or ask a friend to check over your work.

Earlier I discussed how having integrity really involves keeping your word. The words that you choose in your communication have a major impact on how you are perceived by those around you. Language is the most powerful tool we have, so choose wisely. Learn to be articulate and develop your vocabulary. Speak confidently and slowly; think about what you mean and what you are going to say before you start speaking. Be cognizant and aware of how you are being perceived by your audience.

Also, there are a few very important little words that you should aim to master the use of:

> You
> I
> We
> It
> But
> And

The difference between 'you' and 'I' is subtle, but significant. We often make the mistake of using these pronouns incorrectly; projecting what we ourselves think or believe onto others by using the word 'you', when we actually mean 'I'. This can be a cop out. When we're too afraid to say what we really think (I), we frame it according to how we presume others think about it. This seems safer to us. Watch yourself on this one; it's very important. The proper use of 'I' can be profound, while the incorrect use of 'you' can be interpreted as a sign of weakness or a lack of self-confidence.

Also important is distinguishing how you use the terms 'we' and 'I'. We're typically working in team environments and the careful application of these words can see you recognized as a team player versus someone who is out for only their own benefit. Sharing the ownership and recognition of results with the group when appropriate identifies you as a team player. Being tactful and knowing when to personally stand for something using the term 'I' also demonstrates your leadership abilities. It's a careful balance, and be wary of anyone who explicitly uses either term over the other.

'It'. What is 'it'? No one really knows – it's just 'it'. Be extremely careful in your use of this term, which is very easily confused or misconstrued. Where possible, avoid using 'it' as a noun in your verbal and especially written communication. While at times repetitive, the use of the actual noun rather than 'it' makes for much clearer communication and easier decision-making.

The last two words, and possibly the most important ones to distinguish between are 'but' and 'and'. First, here are two definitions:

> **But:** A word used to introduce an idea that is true in spite of either being or seeming contrary to what has just been described.

> **And:** A word used to indicate an additional thing or idea to what has already been stated or described.

These two little words are often used without thought or regard for what they imply. 'But' is a negative word that places limitations on our ideas, as if there is something potentially insurmountable stopping us from achieving what was first said. The word 'and,' however, simply adds two thoughts together without the implications that one thought may have on the other. For example:

I want to start a new initiative at work *but* I don't know where to begin.

I want to start a new initiative at work *and* I don't know where to begin.

The first sentence is self-limiting, while the second is open to possibilities. Try eliminating the word 'but' from your vocabulary and notice what happens to your tone of voice and the feelings that are generated when you replace the word 'but' with the more powerful word 'and.'

Going back to oral communication skills, giving presentations is a popular and effective means of communication in today's workplace. First and foremost, know what you're talking about. If you're unclear about the content of your topic, you'll be lost from the beginning. The ability to cover a large amount of information with a varied audience is a valuable asset. Great presentations are more of a guided conversation than a lecture format. The ability to think on your feet and answer questions is also an important skill to develop.

If you struggle with public speaking or giving presentations, the best way to improve your skills in this area is simply to practice. There are many communications courses you might consider enrolling in, some of which are referenced at the end of this book. You can also ask your peers for feedback and suggestions, or you could consider setting up mock presentations with an audience for practice.

When creating your presentation (or any form of communication for that matter), presence yourself to the purpose of the communication. Why were you asked to analyze this problem? Why is this problem important to management? Which specific findings are more relevant and important to your audience? Anticipate their questions and consider previewing your presentation with the key players individually ahead of time. Outline the next steps for decision-making and assign follow-up actions as appropriate.

Despite the power of language, *how* you speak is often more influential and communicative than the actual words chosen. Your body language and tone of voice can say a lot. Be conscious of how you're presenting your ideas, even ahead of the ideas themselves. You can check out how others are feeling in different situations by reading their body language.

Body language that projects confidence includes standing or sitting tall, leaning into the discussion, and being respectful and engaged when others are speaking. Maintaining eye contact with those you are speaking with is also an indication of self-confidence.

If someone is uninterested in a discussion or idea, they may lean back, cross their arms or legs, or look at the clock multiple times. They may fidget in their seat, adjust their hair or clothes, or look often at their cell phone. Whatever the case, you don't have their attention.

Be conscious of your own body language and what it is communicating to those around you. You may already have developed certain habits, like crossing your arms; or perhaps maintaining eye contact with the people you're talking with is uncomfortable for you. Start to notice these behaviors in your communication and ask yourself how well they are serving you and if they are aligned with the message you're looking to deliver. In some cases, a few simple adjustments can make a world of difference. And don't forget that a genuine smile always goes a long way.

Aim to be clear and concise when articulating your ideas and other verbal communications. Make use of analogies and tailor them to the people you are talking with. Sports analogies are almost always helpful. The ability to think on your feet and spontaneously answer unexpected questions is a valued ability as it demonstrates your understanding of the subject. Remember the Girl Guides motto: 'Be prepared.'[2]

Also, have integrity regarding what you're communicating to others and always honor your word. There is a subtle and very important distinction to

make between saying what you mean and meaning
what you say.

> *"Then you should say what you mean," the March
> Hare went on. "I do," Alice hastily replied; "at least –
> at least I mean what I say – that's the same thing you
> know." "Not the same thing a bit!" said the Hatter.
> "You might just as well say that 'I see what I eat' is the
> same thing as 'I eat what I see'!" "You might just as
> well say," added the March Hare, "that 'I like what I
> get' is the same thing as 'I get what I like'!"*

> – Lewis Carroll, *Alice's Adventures in Wonderland*[3]

Effective communication begins with you and your
choices around how you communicate with others.
Consider that there are four styles of communication:
clear and direct, clear and indirect, masked and direct,
and masked and indirect[4]. All four represent distinct
levels of self-expression and have varying levels of
effectiveness.

Clear and direct communication is the highest
level of self-expression and is the most effective.
Communicating with others clearly and directly
requires a certain level of courage and produces by far
the most effective results. When you are able to fully
express what you think and feel about a situation, you
leave nothing to the imagination, allowing others to
truly understand and appreciate what you are sharing
with them. This type of communication is authentic
and real. It involves being assertive in a healthy way
such that you are able to achieve full self-expression.

In contrast, *clear and indirect communication* occurs when your message is clear but is directed to the wrong or ineffective audience. An example of this is telling your peers at work about how you really feel about a situation or problem at work, but neglecting to share those thoughts with your boss or anyone else who could stand to hear what you have to say and who, more importantly, have the ability to make a difference. Indirect communication often results from a lack of self-confidence or a lack of appreciation regarding how important your own thoughts are to others. Clear and indirect can be a dangerous communication style to regularly engage in because it fundamentally means you've made a choice that effectively violates your own right to self-expression through a failure to be honest with others and with yourself.

Masked and direct communication is often characterized by loud outbursts and seemingly irrational communication. The individual is often confused and frustrated, they are communicating to the correct person but they struggle with the content of their message. This aggressive form of behavior does not achieve effective, workable solutions. Be confused when delivering your message and you'll get confusing results.

Finally, *masked and indirect* communication is the most ineffective form of communication that someone can engage in. This type of communication occurs when both the message and the recipient of your communication are unclear. This passive-aggressive style can get you in trouble quickly.

Clear & Direct	Clear & Indirect
Masked & Direct	Masked & Indirect

Each of these communication styles is a choice, and individuals often move through an evolution in their communication on the way to being clear and direct with their thoughts and feelings. To improve your communication, start by being conscious of the style you tend to default to and evaluate the effectiveness of that style in each situation. Look for opportunities to be brave and shift your communication to as clear and direct a form of self-expression as is possible for you.

Communications soft skills are arguably the most important skills to develop. Whether it's verbal, non-verbal or written communication, put in the effort to develop mastery of these areas and you will be well rewarded.

Chapter 8

Listen Up

Soft Skills Focus: Listening, Openness, Communication and Influence with, and without Authority

Have you ever noticed that when someone is talking to you, that you aren't really listening to them? Instead you're busy interpreting what they're telling you, already thinking about your own reply. Have you ever missed something really important in a conversation because you were so busy thinking about your own response? Your answer to these questions is probably yes, because it's human nature to listen in that way.

Really listening to other people in conversations is a very important skill to develop. The ability to demonstrate listening to what people have to say goes a long way with them. It's through your listening that people see you as being emphatic, expectations are more clearly communicated, and people feel valued for having expressed themselves and for having have been heard by you.

Emphatic listening is listening to really understand and relate to the other person's thoughts and feelings about their situation. Don't assume you know what someone really means. Instead, ask them questions to gain clarity and boost your understanding until you're clear. Repeat what you've heard and understood from the other person in slightly different language to verify your listening. Listen for the underlying emotions and commitments, the part that's not being said. Your effective listening skills will go a long way towards establishing yourself a reputation of being reliable and understanding. When your mutual expectations are clear and well understood, people feel valued in being heard and having their opinion considered.

Listen with the intent to understand, not the intent to reply.

– Stephen Covey[1]

When you have the opportunity to lead or facilitate a group discussion, make note of the participants' body language. Make a concerted effort to ensure everyone contributes to the discussion, which may require you to specifically request the opinions of the quietest individuals. After a strategic decision has been made, look for alignment in what people have said or agreed to with their actions. It is much easier for someone to claim verbal agreement than to act in alignment if they don't actually agree with the direction being taken. If you perceive an issue, have a conversation with the group and inquire into what that individual understands or believes. This action provides the group with the opportunity to see and understand the issue from a different perspective and perhaps alter the direction if warranted.

When dealing with people, remember you are not dealing with creatures of logic, but creatures of emotion.

– Dale Carnegie[2]

When having a private conversation with someone, especially a direct report, it is very important to be present. Eliminate distractions in your office, don't shuffle papers around, don't check your cell phone or read emails, and ignore ringing telephones. Any behavior other than your intent listening is an immediate indication to the other person that you have more important things to do than to listen to what they have to say. If you are waiting for something important, communicate that upfront so they are not taken aback when you suddenly divert your attention. In your conversation, listen attentively to the specific language the person is choosing, resist the urge to interrupt them, and do not finish their sentences for them. If they stumble over their words, provide encouragement so they can effectively express themselves but don't put words in their mouth. Ask them open and leading questions to gain clarity.

If you're looking to improve your listening skills, the first step is to be present with the person you're listening to. Look for opportunities to relate and connect to what they are communicating, and try to imagine what it really feels like to have had the experience they're describing. Use simple and similar language to demonstrate that you are relating and connecting to what they are sharing. Don't have an agenda within your conversations; practice listening to people simply for the sake of authentically connecting with other people.

There is a major difference between hearing what someone says to you and *listening* to what someone says – listening is not the same as hearing. Hearing refers to the sounds that you consciously and unconsciously recognize, while listening is your conscious *comprehension* of those sounds. Listening includes observing how information is conveyed to you from other people, through their tone of voice, body language and the words they choose to use. People give away countless non-verbal clues in their communication, so play close attention to what isn't said. Their facial expressions, the use of sarcasm, their level of engagement and excitement in the conversation, signs that the person is emotionally attached to their message – these are all clues you can pick up on if you're truly looking to understand others. The actual language someone chooses to use only represents a fraction of their communication.

Once, after leading a meeting when I had a particularly bad head cold, I commented to a colleague that I had struggled to hear what everyone was saying in the meeting. It felt like the volume of the world around me had been turned down without my consent. He seemed surprised by my comment, and he relayed how well he thought I had heard what people were saying and effectively incorporated everyone's opinions as the leader of the meeting. I smiled and thanked him for recognizing my listening abilities, a skill I had been actively developing. I'm not sure if he got the difference between hearing and listening that I was alluding to, but personally I took the moment to really appreciate the difference between the two. It was great to see that I could listen to people, even without really being able to hear them. Hearing is what happens when your ears pick up sound waves; listening is how we make sense of those sounds.

Chapter 9

Act Like a Leader

Soft Skills Focus: Vision, Persistence, Listening, Ownership, Assertiveness and Decision-Making

There are many leadership styles you can choose to emulate in your life. No one style is better or worse than another; some just have greater levels of effectiveness when applied in different situations. Common leadership styles include autocratic, democratic, bureaucratic, charismatic, servant and transformative leadership styles[1]. The leadership style I relate to the most is transformational leadership, when your leadership offers positive change to those who follow. Transformational leaders have a strong vision of what is possible; they have high expectations of themselves and of others coupled with an innate ability to motivate other people to act in alignment with their vision. They strive to achieve greatness and ensure that everyone involved benefits from the solution. This type of leadership requires the leader to maintain a high level of personal integrity and demands the ability to hold both themselves and others to account.

As an effective transformational leader, what you do is more important than what you say. In your role, you are representing your vision and what is possible for your organization. Everyone is watching you and they are less likely to choose to follow you if what you do is misaligned with what you say and with your expectations of them. One method to demonstrate the alignment between your actions and your words is to spend a significant amount of your time out in the field, on the shop floor, in the office – wherever the action is. If you want people to be accountable to you, you need to be present and demonstrate a consistent message at all levels, including with yourself. What people see is what you get. If you demonstrate your expectations and your accountability, you have a higher likelihood of seeing the same behaviors in your employees.

As I said, there are many leadership styles, and transformational leadership does not always prove the most successful approach in every situation. Some issues, such as crisis management call for a harder line, for a more directive approach. Every leader will have their default leadership style that is most comfortable and familiar to them; however, great leaders have the ability to use their situational leadership skills to tailor their approach according to the situation. They have learned how to respond in other ways and they know how to play the game.

While I have not yet had the opportunity to fulfill a formal leadership role in my career so far, I've collected many ideas about what great leadership means to me. There are specific behaviors that I feel create highly effective leaders for successful organizations. My collective ideas fall within three main points: being curious, having courage, and being humble.

Leaders who are innately and genuinely curious are always striving to learn more, to grow and get better at their craft. When a leader's authentic curiosity is turned towards their reports, it can instill a strong sense of connection with them and a desire to follow in their direction. Curious leaders are open to the ideas and suggestions of others. Curiosity breeds trust in their relationships with people, and for that reason I believe curiosity is a foundation of great leadership.

I've recognized that having courage and being brave enough to risk what matters most for the sake of growth and improvement is another mark of great leaders. This is most evident during the toughest situations, when they have the most at stake. A leader's courage is also apparent whenever they are able to admit their mistakes and openly demonstrate what they've learned from them. I've noticed that the level of courage displayed by great leaders is directly proportional to their perceived strength of character.

Finally, great leaders are always humble. They understand that they and everyone else are human. Strong leaders demonstrate respect for other people and they are not necessarily always nice. They look for the good in everyone and in all situations while inspiring other people to do the same. Humble leaders make for effective change agents.

So as a young engineer trying to find your way, how do you go about developing your leadership skills? There are likely many opportunities for you right now in your current role if you learn to recognize them. Most young engineers find themselves working in informal leadership roles in their companies, so take advantage of all of these opportunities to practice your leadership skills and develop habits. Whether it's project management, leading team meetings, giving presentations, or even within your everyday interactions with people, all of these tasks are a chance for you to practice being a leader.

Informal leadership relies heavily on influencing others *without* having authority over them, so it provides an even greater challenge if you're willing to accept it and go for it. Look around your organization and notice what's missing; look for ideas that you could tackle in order to create added effectiveness and success. Be mindful of yourself as you assert these ideas and ambitions; don't put yourself in a position where you are neglecting the basic responsibilities of your own current job.

Another great way of developing your leadership potential is to carefully observe others around you and above you in the organization. What types of behavior get recognized and rewarded? What types do not? Look at the behavior patterns of senior leaders in your company. What are they doing that works? What are they doing that doesn't work? Apply what you learn from them and try to emulate the behavior of the leaders you admire.

Great leaders are almost always great simplifiers, who can cut through argument, debate and doubt to offer a solution everybody can understand.

– Colin Powell[2]

At some point (and perhaps it's already happened) you may find yourself in a role where you are managing other people. People are a lot different and much harder to manage than systems and processes. People management requires a very different skill set than tends to be naturally developed in people who have expertise managing systems and processes. Unfortunately, a lot of companies are guilty of confusing that point; they often put good technical people into people leadership roles and the results are less than stellar. Consider that to develop effective people leadership skills, you first need to be good at managing yourself. The people who report to you very easily pick up on your reactions and behaviors, and if you want results from them you have to walk the talk.

One of the qualities of all great leaders is that they not only had a vision; they were also able to effectively share that vision with other people, such that others were inspired. In sharing their ideas and visions with other people, the vision grows as people contribute to them. It is through this process that great leaders are able to enroll others and achieve greatness.

Staying true to that vision and adjusting it as necessary is an important intention to hold as a leader. Pay close attention to how you are acting while in pursuit of your vision, when it's for yourself and especially when it involves others. Notice when you are being stubborn about something and investigate why that is. There is a good chance that there is a specific outcome or process that you are emotionally attached to. Take a step back and really look at yourself in the situation. Consider what it is you're attached to and identify your underlying commitment. Every emotional attachment has an underlying commitment, and once you're able to clearly identify your actual commitment, you're able to drop the emotional attachment and become a much more effective leader. It's about recognizing your own stubbornness and making changes to your behavior to better reflect your actual intentions. *Persistence* is the mature form of being stubborn.

Great leaders are also polite. They have time to say hello and to engage in conversations around the well being of their peers and their employees. They display a genuine interest in other people and really care about others. They're self-aware while also being courteous and respectful of others, regardless of job titles. They're nice to the janitor. Great leaders say please and thank you and really mean it. They avoid gossip, are punctual and hold themselves accountable. In short, they have a great deal of integrity in their behaviors and actions.

When dealing with people, make every effort to remember people's names and use them regularly in conversation. This small effort makes your interactions with them more authentic and more personal, and you're more likely to obtain agreement. If you struggle to remember names, there are a few tricks you can employ to improve your memory. When you're first introduced to someone, repeat their name back to them and immediately use it in a sentence. You can also take a moment and relate their name to the image of someone else you know with the same name, making use of your long term memory to aid your short term memory. If the person you meet has a unique name, ask them to spell it, or ask where it originates from, or what it means. If you can remember enough of their story, you'll be more likely to remember their name. People feel honored when you demonstrate a personal interest in their name.

I'll argue that one of the best traits a leader can demonstrate is to be coachable, meaning that they are truly open to receiving feedback. Leadership, for the most part, is a learned behavior and no one is a perfect leader all the time. One of the strongest skills you can have as a leader is to be honestly open to feedback and to use it constructively in the spirit of continuous improvement. To make this work, you have to actually *listen* to what others have to say and be willing to actively put yourself in uncomfortable situations for the sake of personal growth.

There will be times in your career where you all of a sudden find yourself being looked to as the local "expert" of something you worked on, and you may have no idea how that happened. You somehow became really good at something despite the fact that you really don't enjoy doing that task! The things you are good at and the things you enjoy doing at work will not always be mutually exclusive; unfortunately they can overlap quite a bit. What you do with that is what makes the difference.

When I was in university, we had a pilot plant in the basement of the chemical engineering building. It had various industrial type lab setups down there and students would come and work on group lab projects in the afternoons. In my fourth year, I found myself in a solo lab where I had to design an experiment using the equipment in the basement and then execute my experiment. It was totally backwards from the lab experiments that had been laid out for us in earlier years, a rather foreign concept to a lot of us in the course and an excellent learning opportunity.

I ended up working with a polymer extruding machine, and I designed an experiment using various testing methods to determine the optimal operating conditions for this machine; what temperature to set it at, how much force to apply to the extruder, how much of the polymer pellets to add to the inlet hopper, etc. In the beginning, I had no idea how to work the machine. It was a new piece of equipment in the basement engineering playground and it came with an operating guide. That is, an operating guide originally written in Japanese and poorly translated to English. Instead of labeled buttons with symbols like "ON" or "START," there were random buttons with Japanese pictographs that made very little sense when it came to operating the machine. I assumed the university had gotten a special deal when they purchased this extruder.

It was a nice day outside and I had friends to meet at the pub after my lab, so I was very motivated to complete my self-designed lab experiment in as little time as possible. I start pushing buttons. Stuff happens. Lights come on, it makes noises, and some of the polymer makes it into the molds. I start to learn how it actually works, and eventually (after a few mishaps) I figure out how to make the extruder extrude. I get it to melt the polymer, squeeze it into the molds, and spit out decently formed test pieces. Success! Time to go hang out with my friends! I finish my extruder operating experiment and later handed in my completed report, which as a result of my time spent fooling around with the machine, included a decent operating guide for this very misunderstood piece of equipment.

A few weeks later, the lab coordinator calls me into his office. He's impressed with the fact that I've figured out how to work the extruder, given that other people (university employees) hadn't made much progress. He wants me to create a complete guide for how to operate the extruder and help set up the machine for labs that other students would be completing. A noble idea, but I have one problem with it: I don't enjoy spending my afternoons in the basement of the chemical engineering building and I have enough going on with my other coursework and commitments that I've volunteered for.

In the end I committed to spending a couple of hours showing the actual university employees the basics of how to operate the machine, which again was complete trial and error on my part. We added proper labels to the buttons on the machine in addition to the Japanese pictographs. I pointed out that my trial-by-fire method of operating the machine was an excellent learning exercise for engineering students and we stopped short of developing an actual operating guide. I remember being really annoyed initially at the expectation placed on me to take time out to show others how the extruder worked, but looking back now I see the value in the sharing of my knowledge. While I didn't enjoy the long hours in the basement, I had developed something of value, which needed to be shared.

If you ever find yourself in a similar situation, drop any feelings of being annoyed and thinking only of yourself. Focus instead on how you are sharing your knowledge with other people and making a difference. You're driving results by sharing what you've learned, so harness that power and develop effective training tools to help others succeed in that area. You'll become known as someone willing to help others learn for themselves.

In summary, you don't need a special title to act like a leader. Start now and develop your skills over time. Observe successful leaders and try to emulate their behavior while staying true to yourself. Look for opportunities to play to your strengths and make a difference through your actions.

Leaders are made, they are not born. They are made by hard effort, which is the price which all of us must pay to achieve any goal that is worthwhile.

– Vince Lombardi[3]

Chapter 10

Motivation: Keep Yourself in Gear

Soft Skills Focus: Enthusiasm, Optimism, Persistence and Perseverance

From time to time everyone has experienced a decline in their motivation, whether it's being inconsistent with a habit of working out regularly, eating right, or vowing to break the habit of being just a little bit late for work. So what can you do to maintain your drive and motivation to be your best self?

Engineering problems are tricky, complicated problems that can have a multitude of potential solutions. There will be times at work when you feel incredibly frustrated, when you have been given a seemingly insurmountable problem that appears to have no viable solutions. What makes the difference when dealing with such issues? Persistence. Being persistent is different than being bull-headed or stubborn; it's maintaining the drive for excellence in spite of difficulties, discouragements and indifference. The problem may just take longer to resolve or require a team-based approach or simply a different way of thinking about the problem. Stay committed to solving the problem by reminding yourself of what is at stake if no solution is found. Be tenacious, look for inspiration in others, and ask for help.

When you have exhausted all possibilities, remember this: you haven't.

– Thomas Edison[1]

A great source of motivation is to share your personal and career goals with others. When you are able to share with the people in your life what you're up to and what you want to achieve, you're creating an environment of accountability. Ask other people to routinely come back to you to see how you're advancing towards your goal. You're more likely to complete on what you set out to do when other people are involved. Sometimes the toughest person to give your word to is yourself.

There will be times when you will lose your drive and motivation to complete certain tasks or projects, even though they may once have been important to you. This decline in motivation often follows instances when you've entertained your self-doubt or negative self-talk—that little voice in your head that says you can't actually achieve the outcome you might have thought you could. I relate that voice to the 1984 movie *Gremlins*. The "keep them away from sunlight, don't get them wet, don't feed them after midnight creatures." The gremlins are like that voice in your head that places 'logical' limitations on what's possible for you. In the movie, they eventually killed the gremlins by exposing them to sunlight after getting them wet and feeding them after midnight. In the real world, you can silence the gremlins in your head by simply taking action, accepting responsibility for your actions, and standing for something that really matters to you. It's just that easy.

If you ever get stuck working on an issue or frustrated that what you're doing isn't getting anywhere, remember that engineering problems don't have just one solution. That's why we first thought that being an engineer was cool, remember? Learn to enjoy the journey and stop relating your successes and failures only to the final outcome. Be creative and figure out a solution to your problem.

Logic will get you from A to B.
Imagination will take you everywhere.

– Albert Einstein[2]

When you get clear on what is really important to you, you will find endless amounts of energy and self-created motivation behind the ideas that are aligned with what is really important to you. If your drive or motivation slips, examine why that happened, restore your integrity around the issue, and remember why you started. Go forward again. Don't allow a speed bump to stop you in your tracks.

Following my identity-forming decision at six years old to become an excellent (and seemingly perfect) student, high school came very easy for me. I went to class, listened to the lessons and was able to regularly ace tests without actually needing to study. I breezed through high school and eagerly anticipated going away to university to study engineering. I graduated high school with a 96% average and easily got into Queen's University, but first year engineering was a different story.

I had a lot of fun in university, specifically at the beginning of the first year. It was my first time away from home and there were many new and interesting people and situations to experience. Not realizing that I had severely underdeveloped studying skills from my high school days, I approached my first year engineering courses the same way I had my high school courses. The most challenging course for me in my first term was calculus. There were early indications of failed quizzes and low marks on my assignments, but I figured I could work it out and pass the class. By the time exams came around, I was hopelessly lost in a couple of courses, especially calculus. I tried to study and memorize how to solve the problems but I was *so* lost. I remember struggling to even complete most of the questions on the final calculus exam. The school term ended, we had a big party and everyone went home for the Christmas holidays. Our marks would be available online over the two week holiday.

Looking back, I really had unrealistic expectations when I thought I could pass that calculus exam. I had always been a model student and had no idea how to handle failing a course; it had never been a remote possibility for me. In the end, it all came together on Christmas Eve. My family has a tradition of having a few drinks on Christmas Eve with a light meal and we hang out together by the Christmas tree. I had yet to explain to my parents how the semester had gone for me academically. I was afraid to tell them that I had struggled so much. The results of the calculus exam were playing on my mind, and at one point I decide to get up from the table and go to my bedroom to check my marks online. Not my best move, especially on Christmas Eve. I log into the system and scroll down. There it is, my final mark in calculus: 33%.

I don't know what to do with myself; this has never happened to me before. I close the computer and sit quietly in my bedroom for a few minutes. I eventually go back out to the party without saying anything, find something much harder to drink and drink it much faster than I had been previously. Pretty soon I'm drunk, and my parents definitely notice. Eventually my dad asks me what happened in the bedroom, having recognized a change in my behavior. By now I'm drunk enough that I tell him I failed calculus and I don't know what to do. I expect him to be mad at me and to be disappointed in me. He's funding my university education and I feel like I've let him down. I just failed a whole course in the program I had looked forward to doing for so long.

To my surprise, an odd smile spreads across his face. I'm annoyed that he thinks this is funny. He goes on to explain that he understands how different university is from high school and that he had actually expected me to struggle with it. He then tells me that failing one course in first year is not a big deal and that he had actually failed all of fourth year civil engineering. I was shocked!

He did his best to cheer me up and tried to get me to see that it wasn't the end of the world. His story helped me, but I still felt disappointed with myself and was I was not happy about having to repeat the course.

The holidays continued and as the time approached to go back to school, I realize that I don't want to go back. I had looked forward to going to engineering school, but now that I've realized how hard it is, I'm starting to believe that I'm not good enough to do it and I want to quit. Finally, I get brave enough to approach my dad, again expecting a negative reaction.

Instead, I get a question: "Okay, what's your plan then?" he asks.

"My plan? I don't have a plan. I just don't want to go back because it's too hard," I reply.

He tells me I can study whatever I want in university, but if I'm going to switch programs I need to have a plan first. I get that giving up and just moving home is not an allowable option. I agree to think about other plans and to go back to school and continue with engineering until I have a new plan.

Returning to school, I enrolled in a remedial program called J Section with about 60 other students. The program was designed as a safety net for first year engineering students. They said that if you were smart enough to get into engineering, you were smart enough to stay in engineering. There were six weeks of review from the first term, repeat exams during Reading Week, and then the class began the winter term, running six weeks longer into the summer. It was exactly what I needed.

The teacher for my second attempt at first year calculus was a semi-retired professor named Jim, a man with a huge passion for teaching and for seeing possibility in his students. He was very inspirational and made sure we understood that just because we had failed a course didn't mean we weren't good enough to try again. Jim's fountain-penned, handwritten notes, his Saturday tutorials, his relatable examples, and his commitment to ensuring that everyone really got it was exactly what I needed. Those six extra weeks of school made all the difference for me and totally rebuilt my self-confidence. I completely forgot about creating any sort of new plan for my life. My final mark in calculus round two was 96%. Jim is the reason I stayed in engineering.

I learned a lot from my experiences in first year. I was humbled, realizing I was no longer the top student but still a good enough student to make things work. I learned that sometimes I need to stop and ask for help – something that was very difficult for me to admit. There were highly regarded tutorials offered in the fall during my first attempt at calculus where I could have gotten help had I looked for it. I learned that there is more than one path to success, that some paths are harder than others, and to appreciate the lessons I learned along the way. Looking back now, I wouldn't do it any other way. Making mistakes and failing at things is how I personally learn the best.

Something I've noticed in myself is that I tend to be happiest when I have a challenge that I'm working on, something to work towards that I'm not totally sure I can achieve. I feel more alive when I have something at risk, something that I want to make happen in my life that takes being brave in order to achieve it. I rarely know what the end game looks like but I know that I want to try because it will be exciting, an adventure.

Earlier I said that my sense of adventure had generated in me a secret desire to be an astronaut when I grew up. When I graduated from university, the economy in Alberta was booming. There was so much opportunity for young engineers and new grads in the oil and gas sector and the idea of being a part of that inspired me. An engineering job in Alberta is a far cry from my early ideas of becoming an astronaut but it gave me similar feelings. I considered it an adventure. So when faced with several job offers, two in Ontario (the safe options) or one in Alberta, I chose the exciting one that I didn't immediately know how to do. I decided that I wanted it more than I was afraid of it.

In the year before I graduated from university, I knew that I was going to do something bigger than finish school and go home to get a job in the area where I grew up. While there is nothing wrong with such a choice, I just knew that it wasn't a good fit for me. One of the first times that I realized I was thinking bigger than the small town I grew up in was when I was sixteen years old and first got my driver's license. I decided I needed to have a map in the car so I went to the store to get one. I came home with a map – of Canada. My mom was very surprised, probably at both my larger vision and the sheer impracticality of my purchase. My map of Canada was not going to help me when I was lost on the streets of Belleville, Ontario. I didn't really understand my mother's confusion and replied to her that the store had had a map of the whole world and that I had only bought Canada. I think my Dad later just gave me a map of the local area, which was good because I turned out to be horrible with directions.

When it really came down to choosing to leave Ontario after graduation, I had to decide that I wanted it more than I was afraid of it. I decided to go on an adventure to Alberta because I wanted that experience more than I wanted to stay around home. Before booking my one-way plane ticket, I told myself I always had the option of going back home. I came very close to moving back once, but it's now been eight years and I'm very happy with my choice to risk an adventure.

Everyone has their own risk tolerance that they're comfortable with and they lead their lives accordingly. Many things – your life experiences, your environment, and even the people around you, shape the level of risk that you desire in your life. When weighing options, it can help to consider the probability of occurrence and the magnitude of the potential consequences of your risks. I would encourage you to maintain a healthy amount of risk-taking in your life. Keep yourself challenged but don't get to the point that you can only function on the edge. Taking risks in your life and venturing outside your comfort zone allows you to grow and develop yourself.

Chapter 11

Manage Your Energy, Not Your Time

Soft Skills Focus: Time Management, Self-Awareness and Flexibility

You have the opportunity to have and do anything you want in life; you just can't do *everything*. There are choices to make about what's important to you, and those choices have consequences. Ensuring that you're making conscious choices that are aligned with your values is how you begin to create a sense of balance and fulfillment in your life. When deciding on time management strategies, consider applying your efforts to manage your *energy*, rather than your time.

Energy cannot be created or destroyed; it can only be changed from one form to another.

- Albert Einstein, *Law of Conservation of Energy*[1]

Unlike energy, time is a finite resource; time cannot be stored for later use or changed in form.

Consider that you have infinite energy and finite time. If you take a look at your life, there are two types of activities that you engage in: ones that energize you and ones that wear you down. Knowing this, you can create a plan that maximizes your energy level, and as a result, effectively manage your time.

I've learned that trying to separate my work life and my personal life in my mind is a futile exercise. They're so intertwined that it's easier to consider them as one, and to think about organizing my life as a whole. I think of my life as a series of commitments, and roles that I play within those commitments. I've come to understand the relative importance of the commitments I've created in my life and I've developed boundaries that help to define how much energy I choose to expend in each area.

When considering your daily activities, it's likely that you can already identify which activities energize you and which ones drain your energy. When you must complete what you experience as an energy-sucking activity, avoid dodging the responsibility for it and simply manage it away by balancing it out with energy generating activities.

You might be inclined to work extra hours in the name of getting ahead at work or more honestly, looking good in the eyes of your employer. Realistically, the company you work for will always support your working extra hours, but in doing so, you introduce the potential opportunity to become resentful of your job over time, particularly if you aren't managing to stay true to yourself along the way. If working extra hours leaves you feeling fulfilled and energized, then great. But if working overtime doesn't make you happy, look at what you might be able to do differently to achieve the feeling of fulfillment and contribution in your work. Remember that you always have a *choice* (no matter how impossible life seems) and that you can alter your situation if you're not happy with it. Look for other opportunities within the organization if you like the company, or outside of the organization if you don't like the direction of the company.

When laying out your schedule, consider all of the activities you have going on in your life as a whole. Develop an appreciation of which activities energize you and which activities deplete your energy, and then aim to balance them out to achieve emotional satisfaction in your life. There's only so much time in a day or a week, and I've found that this approach allows me to be more conscious of managing my priorities, and in doing so I'm able to achieve balance in my life.

It's amazing how much time we can lose to procrastination in our lives. Understanding what's *most important* to you goes a long way to replacing procrastination with inspired actions. There is only so much time, so it's important to realize the impact of procrastination in your life and particularly on the things you claim to be important to you. Whenever I get stuck on a task, I relate it back to my commitments in life and how important they are to me. I look to remember why I started and through that, I rediscover my inspiration and the motivation to continue. Focus on being present in whatever you are doing as a sure way to eliminate thoughts of procrastination.

In life we tend to relate to tasks and activities as being either urgent or important. We then have a tendency to take action to complete the urgent things over the important things, probably because they are more immediate. Depending on your role, these urgent and reactive tasks might constitute a large portion of your job or your life. Notice that the important things don't disappear or go away while the urgent things are being taken care of. They actually accumulate. Without action to complete the important tasks, you can develop a feeling of dissatisfaction, of not being able to work on anything important because you're constantly distracted by what is considered urgent. To maintain balance in your life, it's necessary to work on both the urgent and important aspects of your life. The relative split between the two may not always be equal or constant but it's essential to be in action in both areas.

Additionally, in our work and in life there are certain tasks and assignments that must be done but that we find boring, uninspiring or basically useless. These activities suck energy from us and leave us feeling tired. Since some of these activities are definitely required, why make them harder to complete than they need to be? Consider making them somehow interesting or fun instead of boring or dreadful, create a game to complete the boring tasks. Use your imagination and look for the good in everything that you do.

In every job that must be done, there is an element of fun.

– Mary Poppins[2]

Chapter 12

Plays Well With Others

Soft Skills Focus: Teamwork, Being Inclusive,
Communication and Listening

Knowing how to work effectively as part of a team is essential to your success. You can be the smartest, most capable individual, but if you don't harness the power of teams, your ultimate level of success will be extremely limited.

> *You can design and create, and build the*
> *most wonderful place in the world. But it*
> *takes people to make the dream a reality.*

> – Walt Disney[1]

To be considered an effective team player, you first need to be open to the backgrounds, opinions, and ideas of other people. While you likely have your own ideas of how the team should tackle a project or a problem, don't limit yourself by thinking that your idea is superior or the only way to create the desired results. An effective team can create levels of success that you could never achieve on your own. The ability to work with people from diverse backgrounds is an important asset. There will be differences of opinion and understanding between you and your teammates, so the ability to work with differences is vital to creating an environment that will facilitate the success of the team.

When building a new team, the leader should look to the various skill sets that are required for the success of the team. Ideally, they would then staff the team to meet that criterion rather than filling the team by designated roles. To truly be successful, teams need to develop mutual accountability, and team members need to trust and be accountable to each other, as well as to the team leader.

Never underestimate the importance of having well defined roles and responsibilities for your teams. It is imperative that the purpose and goals of the team are effectively communicated and understood by all team members and also by everyone the team interacts with. If these concepts are not crystal clear to everyone involved (directly or indirectly), your team will falter. If you are not the leader of your group and you perceive an issue regarding unclear roles and responsibilities, you should raise it with the group leader. Share with them the direct impact this ambiguity is having on your effectiveness in what you understand your role to be and what you perceive could be possible for the group if clarity was established. Make a request of them to improve the team's understanding of their roles.

Even the most effective team members can become discouraged and disengaged if they don't feel that they are making positive contributions towards the common goal. To combat complacency within the group, celebrate the small wins and the large wins. Show exactly how the accomplishment ties to the overall goal of the team and the positive impact it has. This might seem like a waste of time or an unnecessary extra task, but it can go a very long way in maintaining the motivation of the group. Celebrating the small wins is of particular importance if the group morale is low. People like to know that they're on track and perceived to be on the right track by others. When I was the interim leader of the daily operations group for the plant, we faced a strenuous time during a long maintenance outage. The group's motivation was on the decline, so I created a running list to capture all of the small wins our group was achieving. The list grew over several weeks and each team member contributed to it, thereby rediscovering their motivation and achieving a sense of fulfillment knowing that they were on the road to achieving the goals we had set.

Chapter 13

Find Your Balance

Soft Skills Focus: Balance, Flexibility and Time Management

As we begin to find our way in the real world, I believe the thing we're really searching for and then trying to maintain is *a sense of balance* in our lives. Remember back to when you were first learning to ride a bike and had to learn to find your balance. You kept trying and kept trying until one day, all of a sudden, it just worked! Finding your balance in life works similarly. Your main method of learning is still trial and error. Finding your balance might come fairly easy for you, but keeping it and maintaining that feeling can be fleeting. Once you have found it for good, you definitely know it – everything in your life just starts to work.

Step with care and great tact, and remember
that Life's a great Balancing Act.

– Dr. Seuss, *Oh, The Places You'll Go!*[1]

The first idea that really helped me when it came to finding my balance was to give up on trying to be *perfect*, to simply just do my best in whatever I was doing. Doing something perfectly and doing something well enough (again, a code word for giving your best effort) create two very different ways of being. True perfection does not exist, so to always expect that of yourself is a sure way to prevent yourself from enjoying the feeling of balance in your life. Trying to be perfect all the time will wear you out. Perfection is like a trap, while having the expectation to just do your best, whatever that looks like, is a key component to achieving balance.

Another foundational way of developing your sense of balance is to set boundaries for yourself and to effectively communicate those boundaries to other people in your life. Don't allow yourself to compare what you're doing to that of those around you. I used to have an idea in my head that when other people left work early or even on time to pick up their kids from daycare, that I obviously needed to stay back, work longer hours and make up for their absence. Not a particularly balanced life decision for myself at the time.

At some point I realized that: one, I wasn't really that imperative to the operation; and two, if I continued this behavior, I would never have any kids of my own to go and pick up! My current life priorities didn't involve children, but that didn't diminish the things I was committed to in my life. I still had personal commitments; we all do. Recognizing this, I started to leave work on time and go to the gym – a much more balanced life decision.

There's no such thing as work-life balance.
There are work-life choices, and you make them,
and they have consequences.

– Jack Welch[2]

A simple exercise that can help you to get clear on your commitments in life is to write them out on paper. Prioritize them and know which ones you're willing, and not willing, to compromise on in the short term. Examine the roles you play within those commitments and see how well they fit together. Are there any underlying themes? This exercise can help you to understand your larger purpose, and what you're all about. When I completed this exercise myself, I saw that all of my commitments share the common theme of wanting to help other people see what's possible for themselves and their lives. It's a game that I've committed to playing that I call "Everybody Gets Their Own Greatness." Whenever I get stuck in life, I go back to the intent of this game I created and look to see what's missing and how I can find my way out of being stuck. What kind of game would you like to play?

Many people today, not exclusive to us engineers, have developed a skewed idea of what it means to be truly happy with life. People frequently mistake happiness for the things they have and the things they are doing in their lives when really they're confusing happiness with pleasure. Pleasure is the act of doing things you enjoy, which might make you happy – until you stop doing the things that are providing pleasure. Happiness achieved through pleasure is a fleeting feeling; it doesn't persist once your enjoyable activity ends. Happiness is really about *who you are being*. True happiness is discovered when your actions are consistent with who you are being, that is, with your authentic self.

It is important to develop hobbies and interests for yourself outside of your job. These will help to recharge your energy when work consumes your energy, and they will make you a well-rounded individual. They may even provide you with the opportunity to set some ambitious personal goals – photography and downhill skiing are two of mine. You may choose to play a musical instrument, learn another language, take part in sports and other physical activities, read, learn to cook, or join a non-profit organization. Find something that interests you or that you've always thought you'd like to try but haven't gotten around to it. Invite a friend to join you in a new activity or adventure. Look to understand your unique skills and strengths and then apply them in your life. If you start something and it doesn't work out, there are endless other choices. Keep growing and actively developing yourself. What if you even fail at something? Not a problem. Dust yourself off and try something else; there are endless opportunities.

In the pursuit of achieving balance in your life, it is important to consider the influence of your workplace climate. 'Workplace climate' includes things such as having strong visionary leadership, growth and development opportunities for employees, and the level of workload and expectations placed on workers. To evaluate the current climate of your workplace, ask yourself some questions. Do your personal values match those of your organization? Which types of behaviors are rewarded in your company? Are you willing to play the level of game that is expected? How does the culture of the organization play into the company's decisions and structure? What level of risk is the organization comfortable with? When these ideas are in harmony and aligned with your own authentic way of being, it is much easier to achieve balance in your life. When they are misaligned, you may find it harder to attain results, you may feel stressed, and your life balance is more likely to remain elusive. The climate of your workplace can change over time as things like leadership and business needs and priorities change, or it can remain much the same. Whichever is the case, the 'climate' you work in is something to be aware of and, if possible, strive to influence in a positive direction.

Ultimately, finding your balance is about being aware of your level of emotional satisfaction and striving to be emotionally satisfied with your life. Balance takes work to achieve, as you often have to address underlying issues that may not even be visible to you when you first set out on this path. Understand what is really important to you and set boundaries around those areas of your life. Manage your energy and communicate the boundaries you have set with other people in your life. Continually reevaluate them as you may choose to adjust them over time. Create a schedule and stick to it so you develop healthy habits. Schedule time for play and having fun because life is not all about work.

Chapter 14

Learn From The Best:
The Power of Mentoring

Soft Skills Focus: Openness, Having a Growth Mindset, and Being Self-Aware

Mentoring is the act of sharing knowledge and experiences. Typically, an experienced individual (mentor) provides advice or guidance to a younger, less experienced individual (protégé) in an area where the mentor has developed a level of expertise. When a mentoring relationship works well, it can provide exceptional value to the protégé and also to the mentor. Great mentors can see your potential, even when you may not see it yourself. They will ask you leading questions and help you to recognize both your strengths and the areas where you can learn and improve. Mentors are typically a source of inspiration and motivation because they see you as bigger than you are, and have the ability to view your situation from the outside as someone who has experience and wisdom to offer.

A mentor is someone who allows you
to see the hope inside yourself.

– Oprah Winfrey[1]

As a young engineer, one of the best ways to develop your soft skills is to create a mentoring relationship with a more experienced professional in your field. The first step is to find a mentor to work with. Many companies offer formal mentorship programs that pair you with senior employees. Or you can search out individuals that you respect and admire and ask them if they would be willing to mentor you.

A highly effective way to approach life is to believe that you have something valuable to learn from every person you encounter in your life. Mentoring relationships are about taking actions to develop yourself by discussing your performance with someone you admire and respect. I would encourage you to look past your 'comfort zone' when selecting a mentor. Some of the best mentors are the ones who have well developed skills that lie outside of your comfort zone, the ones you're already naturally great at.

When you're looking for a mentor, consider that there are specific qualities that will make some people better mentors than others. Look for someone who demonstrates a high level of personal integrity and with whom you share common values. Observe how they interact with people in their job because you want to work with someone who is genuinely interested in sharing their skills and experiences with others. Some qualities to look for when selecting someone to approach to become your mentor include integrity (as mentioned), self-awareness, openness and optimism. Also, someone who easily sees past roadblocks to find solutions has more to offer you than someone who has difficulty with adversity or challenges. Obviously you want to look for someone who has been successful in a similar area to the one that you are interested in and has done so in a way that you admire and respect. Great mentors are good listeners and are compassionate in their communication. They're also straight with people, meaning that they will be able to effectively tell you what you need to hear in order to grow and improve your soft skills.

On the other side of the equation, there are also qualities and attributes that make for a great protégé. To get the most out of your relationship you're your mentor, you should be engaged in and excited about your self-development. Be curious and genuinely interested in what your mentor has to offer from their life experiences. A certain level of self-awareness is important; if you understand your current limitations and areas where you would like to improve, this will provide your mentor a basis to work from. Always be respectful of your mentor's time and be actively engaged in your conversations with them. Remember that as the protégé in the relationship, you're responsible for both your own success and the success of the mentoring agreement. Lay some ground rules at the beginning of the relationship: establish the frequency and length of your meetings and schedule them in your calendar. Ask how you can best contact your mentor outside of those scheduled times should something come up for you that you want to discuss with them. Take on the responsibility of having the mentoring relationship work for both of you.

Once you've established a mentoring relationship, what should you talk about with your mentor? With so many possible opportunities and uncertainties, this initial discussion could seem rather daunting, especially if an area you're looking to improve on is self-confidence. First, make an effort to learn what they're about and what they're committed to in their lives and in their careers. Ask them what they like to do outside of work, and look to find out what motivates and drives them to be successful. Share with them how their views relate to yours and look to find opportunities through these discussions for your own personal growth. To get the most out of your mentor's guidance, you need to be vulnerable with them and share what you see are your bigger weaknesses or areas for growth, and let them know you are committed to improve.

Ask your mentor about the path they took to arrive at their current role and what they learned about themselves along the way. Was there anything that they wish they had known or figured out earlier in their career? Get them to share their success stories as well as the moments that didn't go very well, and find out what they learned from those situations. If they're open to being very straight with you, consider asking them what their biggest weakness used to be and what they did to overcome it. How were they able to first distinguish that for themselves, and then what did they do to make a positive difference in that area of their life? You could even ask them what areas of self-improvement they are currently working on.

Finally, one of my favorite questions to ask my mentors is what *I* can do to help *them*. It's often unexpected and can catch people off guard, as it flips the general context of mentoring on its head. In authentically asking this question, you're demonstrating your genuine interest and commitment to the mentoring relationship and having it really work for both people. You may even be surprised in what your mentor chooses to request your assistance with. Remember that there is really no end point to arrive at in terms of developing soft skills; everyone is simply out to improve their skills over time, to develop mastery of their craft.

I've been lucky enough to have had several excellent mentors in my career so far. They have each offered great advice and guidance, and helped to shape my career and in some cases, the direction of my life. They have helped me to discover for myself what is really most important to me, and what I'm truly passionate about. I highly encourage you to seek out the people in your company, in your industry, and in your life that you respect and admire, and then ask them if they would be willing to begin a mentoring relationship with you.

Chapter 15

Putting It All Together:
Engineering Possibilities

Soft skills are truly the difference makers when it comes to predicting the success of one engineer compared to another. More importantly, well developed soft skills, and self-awareness in particular, are the markers of individuals who succeed in achieving balance in their lives. Knowing what is most important in your life, continually standing for those things, and having well established and well communicated boundaries are key to success in this area.

This book was written out of the possibility of compassion and connection; I was looking to share my newfound understanding of myself and my life in a way that would inspire other young engineers to see what is possible for themselves and to inspire them to pursue what they are most passionate about in their life. Of all the concepts and tools presented, developing self-awareness and self-confidence, demonstrating integrity, and bring true to your authentic self are really at the core of my message. The masterful combination—Integrity, Leadership, Power, Influence and Continuous Improvement soft skills—are what will make the difference for you in your career and, more importantly, in your life.

Remember that you have the power to choose your own attitude in life, thereby choosing your own adventure in life. Resist the habit of spinning your wheels, of over-analyzing everything that goes on around you, and just be okay with it all. Understand which areas you are able to effectively influence and don't fret over the ones over which you have no control. Actively work to develop your communication and listening skills to effectively interact with people.

You can talk about or worry about things in life as long as you want, but know that the only thing that will make any difference is to *take action* in that area of your life. The most important areas are often the scariest, so be brave and do it anyway. Dare to be great. Consider that knowing what to do is only part of the equation; it's only taking action that produces results. Do the work, get authentically connected to what really matters to you, and take inspired actions to achieve whatever it is that you see possible for your life. The only one stopping you is very likely yourself.

Believe that you can do it and you will do it. Take actions consistent with what you're out to create for yourself and for the world and your possibilities will turn into reality.

Take chances, make mistakes, get messy.

– Ms. Frizzle, *The Magic School Bus*[1]

I wrote this book out of the inspiration of my own journey, collecting everything I have earned along the way and all that I wish I had known earlier in my life, and sharing it in a way that I hope is relatable to other young engineers. In writing this book, it may seem like I have it all figured out. Know that this is not the case; I'm still actively engaged in learning more, in developing and improving myself, and I am committed to do so for the rest of my life. With all that I've learned and shared in this book, I challenge you to commit to your own curiosity for the sake of discovering what else just might be possible.

If ever there is a tomorrow when we're not together – there is something you must always remember. You are braver than you believe, stronger than you seem and smarter than you think. But the most important thing is, even if we're apart...I'll always be with you.

– A.A. Milne, *Winnie the Pooh to Christopher Robin*[2]

Resources

There are several remarkable programs and references available to you to further your soft skills development. Some ideas and examples include:

- The Landmark Curriculum for Living (www.landmarkworldwide.com)
- The Dale Carnegie Course
- Toastmasters (find your local chapter)
- Seven Habits of Highly Effective People by Stephen Covey
- Unstuck Digital Coach (www.unstuck.com)
- MindTools (www.mindtools.com)
- Volunteering for causes that are important to you
- Reading biographies of people you are inspired by
- Professional Development programs offered by your local Professional Engineering Association

Works Cited

What's Possible?

1. "Maya Angelou." BrainyQuote.com. Xplore Inc, 2015. 31 May
   2015.
   http://www.brainyquote.com/quotes/quotes/m/mayaangelo101
   310.html

Discovering Your Passions

1. Williams, Margery. *The Velveteen Rabbit.* New York: Bantam
   Doubleday Dell Publishing Group, Inc., 1922. 5 – 8. Print.

2. "Chris Hadfield." Goodreads.com. Gooodreads Inc, 2015. 31
   May 2015.
   https://www.goodreads.com/author/quotes/1136925.Chris_Had
   field

The Difference Makers: Soft Skills for Engineers

1. *The Wizard of Oz.* Dir. Victor Fleming. Metro_Goldwyn-
   Mayer, 1939. Film.

What Do You Want To Be When You Grow Up?

1. *Alice's Adventures in Wonderland.* Lewis Carroll. New York:
   MacMillan, 1865. Print. 49-50.

2. Doran, et al. "There's a S.M.A.R.T. way to write
   management's goals and objectives." *Issue of Management
   Review* 70.11 (1981)

Learn To Manage Yourself First

1. "Albert Einstein." BrainyQuote.com. Xplore Inc, 2015. 31
   May 2015.
   http://www.brainyquote.com/quotes/quotes/a/alberteins118979.h
   tml

2. "Carlos Castaneda." BrainyQuote.com. Xplore Inc, 2015. 31
   May 2015.
   http://www.brainyquote.com/quotes/quotes/c/carloscast164498.h
   tml

3. "Albert Einstein." BrainyQuote.com. Xplore Inc, 2015. 31 May 2015.
http://www.brainyquote.com/quotes/quotes/a/alberteins133991.html

4. "Dale Carnegie." wisdomquotes.com, 2015. 31 May 2015.
http://www.wisdomquotes.com/quote/dale-carnegie-1.html

5. "Werner Erhard." Blog.gaiam.com, Gaiam Inc, 2015. 31 May 2015.
http://blog.gaiam.com/quotes/authors/werner-erhard

Understand Your Generational Identity

1. "Albert Einstein." BrainyQuote.com. Xplore Inc, 2015. 31 May 2015.
http://www.brainyquote.com/quotes/quotes/a/alberteins148778.html

Operate With Integrity

1. "Walt Disney." BrainyQuote.com. Xplore Inc, 2015. 31 May 2015.
http://www.brainyquote.com/quotes/quotes/w/waltdisney100644.html

2. "Isaac Newton." BrainyQuote.com. Xplore Inc, 2015. 31 May 2015.
http://www.brainyquote.com/quotes/quotes/i/isaacnewto382602.html

3. "Stephen Covey." BrainyQuote.com. Xplore Inc, 2015. 31 May 2015.
http://www.brainyquote.com/quotes/quotes/s/stephencov636489.html

Communicate!

1. "Albert Einstein." BrainyQuote.com. Xplore Inc, 2015. 31 May 2015.
http://www.brainyquote.com/quotes/quotes/a/alberteins383803.html

2. "Guides." Girl Guides of Canada, 2012. 9 June 2015.
   https://www.girlguides.ca/WEB/GGC/Programs/Core_Progra
   mming/Guides/GGC/Programs/Core_Programming/Guides.asp
   x?hkey=8db66b05-e766-4bcf-9776-8144376b206b

3. *Alice's Adventures in Wonderland.* Lewis Carroll. New York:
   MacMillan, 1865. Print. 54.

4. Epstein, N. B., Bishop, D., Ryan, C., Miller, & Keitner, G.
   "The McMaster Model View of Healthy Family Functioning."
   Normal Family Processes. Eds. In Froma Walsh. New
   York/London: The Guilford Press, 1993. 138 – 160. Print.

Listen Up

1. "Stephen Covey." BrainyQuote.com. Xplore Inc, 2015. 31 May
   2015.
   http://www.brainyquote.com/quotes/quotes/s/stephencov63650
   8.html

2. "Dale Carnegie." BrainyQuote.com. Xplore Inc, 2015. 31 May
   2015.
   ahttp://www.brainyquote.com/quotes/quotes/d/dalecarneg1307
   27.html

Act Like a Leader

1. Manktelow, James, and Any Carlson. "Leadership Styles:
   Choosing the Right Approach for the Situation."
   MindTools.com. Mind Tools Ltd, 1996-2015. Web. 9 June
   2014.
   http://www.mindtools.com/pages/article/newLDR_84.htm

2. "Colin Powell." BrainyQuote.com. Xplore Inc, 2015. 31 May
   2015.
   http://www.brainyquote.com/quotes/quotes/c/colinpowel14499
   2.html

3. "Vince Lombardi." VinceLombardi.com. Family of Vince
   Lombardi c/o Luminary Group LLC, 2010. 31 May 2015.
   http://www.vincelombardi.com/quotes.html

Motivation: Keep Yourself In Gear

1. "Thomas A. Edison." Goodreads.com. Gooodreads Inc, 2015.
   31 May 2015.

http://www.goodreads.com/quotes/97717-when-you-have-exhausted-all-possibilities-remember-this---you

2. "Albert Einstein." BrainyQuote.com. Xplore Inc, 2015. 31 May 2015. http://www.brainyquote.com/quotes/quotes/a/alberteins121643.html

Manage Your Energy, Not Your Time
1. "Albert Einstein." Goodreads.com. Goodreads Inc, 2015. 31 May 2015. http://www.goodreads.com/quotes/4455-energy-cannot-be-created-or-destroyed-it-can-only-be

2. *Mary Poppins*. Dir. Robert Stevenson. Walt Disney, 1964. Film.

Plays Well With Others
1. "Walt Disney." Disney.com. Disney, 2014. 31 May 2015. http://www.disneyanimation.com/studio/studiolife

Find Your Balance
1. *Oh, The Places You'll Go!*. Dr. Seuss. New York: Random House, 1990. Print.

2. Welch, Jack. Speech at the Society for Human Resource Management Annual Conference. New Orleans. 28 June 2009. Address.

Learn From the Best: The Power of Mentoring
1. "Oprah Winfrey." blog.geteverwise.com. Everwise Corporation, 2015. 31 May 2015. http://blog.geteverwise.com/20-inspiring-mentoring-quotes

Putting It All Together: Engineering Possibilities
1. *The Magic School Bus*. Scholastic Entertainment. PBS, 1994 – 1998.

2. Milne, A. A. *Winnie-the-Pooh*. New York: Puffin Books, Reissue edition 2005. Print.

About the Author

Holly Blair is a chemical engineer currently living and working in Calgary, Alberta. After graduating in 2007 from Queen's University in Kingston, Ontario, she spent the first several years of her career working as a process engineer at chemical plants in Alberta. Innately curious and interested in how things work, Holly enjoys downhill skiing, travel and photography, thereby fulfilling her desire for adventure. As a bold leader and an engineer who gets people, she has a true passion for coaching and developing people. She is committed to making a real difference for engineers and young professionals in the early stages of their careers, helping young people achieve balance in their lives while pursuing what is most important to them in life.